TENDING
THE TEMPLE

...my journey

*A guide to balance, empowerment and healing from the inside out ~
Includes 80 healthy recipes and shopping guide*

PATRICIA G. MAGYAR

CreateSpace, North Charleston, South Carolina
Copyright © 2011 Patricia G. Magyar

ISBN-10: 1456304283
EAN-13: 9781456304287
Library of Congress Control Number: 2011905324

CONTENTS

INTRODUCTION

My purpose is to help and empower all who read this book–to demonstrate the power of balance and simplicity in your life; to show you practical ways to restore harmony within you and in your home. Faith and nutrition greatly affect your quality of life. You truly are what you eat, think and believe. It is my sincere hope, that what I share will energize you to make changes that lead to healing and peace. Please allow my journey to help you help yourself, because when our physical and spiritual health suffers, everything else does.

Years ago, I volunteered to teach children's church to pre-K children. I began a new season in life because my youngest was entering that class. Each Sunday morning I observed their emotional state as they walked through my door. I taught during the 8:30 a.m. service, and to be honest, I dreaded when certain children came. The few kids who were half asleep were easier to handle than the children that were *pinging* off the walls. It seemed to be the same ones every week. I often asked the *wall pingers* what they ate for breakfast. The answers of these four and five year olds amazed me. At this point in my life I had been studying nutrition for approximately eight years. So hearing about their poisonous menus broke my heart. They happily informed me of the doughnuts, chocolate bars, fast food, soda and Mom's coffee that they consumed. Ugh! What are these parents trying to do, fill a hole or nourish a child? The calmer kids would often say things like, "Mom made me eggs or pancakes" or "I had a banana in the car." Hurray for the banana kids mom!

Let's celebrate the banana here for a moment. It's cheap and nutritious, high in potassium, low in fat, filling and it comes in its own package. Now, you can't say that about many foods. So, let's get back to the *wall pingers*. It was all I could do to get those kids settled down in order to teach them. For the record, I didn't blame them, I felt sorry for them. I blamed the parents who didn't know any better or who just didn't care.

Most parents make the *time* and/or *money* excuse when it comes to feeding their families nutritious foods. I have come to realize this cold hard fact over the years . . . if you don't make time for your health now, you will be forced to later. "Healthy foods are too expensive," I often hear. But I know they're not as expensive as hospitals. This book is my way of being silent no more. It is for the child who can't focus in school and the parent who is beyond frustration. It is for the couple so easily irritated with one another that they are drifting apart. It is for the self-destructive teen who hates her parents and herself and doesn't know why.

There is something you can do about these problems. It is *never* too late. The very next moment is new to you, so take it and run with it. Reading about my own personal journey is your first step. It will enlighten you, empower you and guide you in what to do next. My hope–and expectancy– is that you'll have happier and healthier days ahead. The choice is yours.

And so it begins . . .

It's September 1990–and it's a girl! At twenty-four I had been married three years, and now for the first time I was a mother. Life as I knew it would never be the same. I nursed my first-born exclusively for the first six months. After all, my body was designed for the task. So I figured it must be what was best for her. The fact that it helped me to return to my pre-baby weight was a big plus too. My milk was like watered-down skim milk. I did not take care of myself as I should have throughout my pregnancy. Now don't get me wrong, I wasn't smoking or drinking. I took my prenatal vitamins and ate what I wanted to. My OB-GYN did not teach me anything about a healthy pregnancy diet, so I did what I thought best at the time.

At the age of 3 months–and shortly after her first round of immunizations–my daughter came down with severe eczema on most of her body. She was red and crusty in most of the folds of her little body. As a new mom this was devastating to me. I took her to the pediatrician, and he gave me a prescription for a type of cortisone cream. He did not tell me that it was a steroid. He did, however, tell me to use it sparingly. So I applied a thin layer on all of the red spots, and the next day the rash was almost gone. The drug cleared her eczema. I was so thrilled to see her skin soft and healthy looking again.

But, the thrill turned to dread when the eczema returned a few days later. You see, symptoms are designed by our Creator to tell us two things: We are *toxic* or we are *deficient*. We are toxic because we have put poisons into our bodies and deficient because we lack nutrients. The drug merely masked the symptoms but the root cause was not addressed. So I continued to use the steroid cream. The pediatrician had no alternative or recommendations. But he said hopefully she'd outgrow it. One day I decided to investigate the ingredients in the cream. To my horror I learned of all the warnings for steroid use. I immediately discontinued putting that poison on my baby girl.

Throughout this entire time I prayed to God for answers. "Heal my baby girl, Lord, and lead me to what I'm supposed to do to help her. What is my part?" One morning, I was listening to Christian radio, and the host had a guest doctor on who talked about nutrition. My ears perked up and I listened intently. I wrote down all his information and bought his literature. He was a biologist and nutritionist with his own medical practice. He taught Biblical nutrition and the Levitical diet of clean and unclean foods (Leviticus 11). I soon found myself absorbing a whole new way of thinking. I thanked God as I shared with my husband what I had learned, because he was on board with me. There is nothing more powerful when two or more are in agreement. Hurray! A partner to help, pray and share the parental burden of caring for healthy offspring.

The very next thing we did was to go through our cabinets and read the ingredient labels. We got rid of everything that had chemicals, preservatives, additives, colors, artificial flavoring and the like. We cleaned out all of the unclean food in our refrigerator like pork and shellfish. You see, the nutritionist taught that if God told the Israelites not to eat it, it must have been for a good reason. We soon found our cupboards bare. We then replaced harmful foods with God-made foods that had God-made ingredients. Along with our daughter, both my husband and I have had a few of our own physical ailments. He lived for years with allergies–shooting up his thighs with allergy shots and popping a host of rainbow-colored pills. I, on the other hand, suffered with constipation, irregular periods and PMS.

But as we began to implement our new healthy lifestyle, we experienced a significant improvement. Our little girl's eczema lightened and disappeared on some parts of her body, but not all. That wasn't good enough for me. When my diet improved, my milk went from watered-down skim milk to half-and-half.

So, there it is . . . the beginning of my journey. I was determined to rectify the situation as soon as possible. It was difficult as I learned of all the external things I had to do to alleviate her condition. I could not dress her in lace dresses; she was comfortable in plain 100% cotton clothes. (I was a brand new mom and so wanted the pink lace and frills.) I also learned that perfumes, powders and lotions could aggravate the eczema. Oh, how I prayed that the eczema would just disappear and never return. One time I remember praying my most fervent prayer over her while she slept. I believed by faith, that when I opened my eyes the eczema would be no more.

However, hind-sight is 20-20. Now I know the Lord was preparing me for this nutrition ministry. If the eczema had been miraculously taken from her, I would not have pursued nutrition at all. Of course, I didn't know then and I grew frustrated with unanswered prayer and a pediatrician who offered no remedy. I began to dig deeper and read all I could get my hands on, thus building a good-sized library.

I recall a time when my daughter, who was a slender little girl, came down with a belly bug. She was about eighteen months old and she couldn't hold down food. She did not have a fever, just vomiting. She would hold down just a bit of food and after a short while, she'd toss it up again. Since she was a slender toddler, I worried over possible weight loss. Her emotional state was happy and normal and she had no pain, so I wasn't worried about anything major.

This episode happened over a weekend, so early Monday morning I had her in the pediatrician's office. The doctor told me that she had a virus and to keep her hydrated, but there was nothing else to do. I asked him how long until she was well. He snickered and told me about a child who'd been vomiting for thirteen days. Ugh, my baby was already thin. What would thirteen days do to her? She'd disappear! Again there were no solutions and no active participation in getting to the root of the problem. I wanted to take a proactive role in my daughter's healing so I investigated alternative medicine. This led me to a chiropractor who used herbs and supplements to help the body help itself. I made an appointment with him. We discussed the cause of her ailment and a natural treatment procedure. He sent me home with a barley grass drink and a combination of herbal supplements. Arriving home, I started her on the regime with a little apple sauce and tiny sips of purified water. I was told to repeat the process every two hours. Within six hours she was holding down her baby food and never vomited again. Over and over again natural remedies, along with diet change improved my family's health. I continued to search for better ways to eat, think and live.

I had a friend who was diagnosed with leukemia at thirty-nine. Approximately five years prior, I buried my mother who was only fifty-one. She had the same disease. I took it upon myself to compare Mom and my girlfriend's diets and lifestyle. I found many surprising similarities. Both women grew up without a personal relationship with Jesus Christ. Each of them led a worldly lifestyle for many years. Both ladies drank, smoked, used artificial sweeteners, drank a lot of coffee, had hysterectomies, tonsillectomies, appendectomies, dyed their hair . . . and the list went on. Wow, could it be coincidence that they died of the same disease? I don't think so.

During my friend's battle with cancer she went on an all-raw diet, which included large amounts of raw vegetable juices and no meat. For the short time that she adopted this diet, she told me she felt better than she had in years. You see, I don't want to bury anyone else prematurely! Instead, I want to share with the world how to live preventatively. Then you may never have to hear, "You've got cancer, MS, diabetes . . ."

About ten years ago another friend had her fourth child. At about six months old, this child could not hold down solid foods. My friend did what any concerned mom does; she took her to the pediatrician. He referred her to another doctor, who told her that her baby had a detached colon. Moreover, he needed to do exploratory surgery right away. My girlfriend was beside herself! He wanted to cut that little girl in half to see if her colon was detached. She immediately asked for a second opinion and the doctor—in so many words—told her that she'd be killing her child if she didn't do the surgery immediately.

Being a smart woman, she drove to the next big city and got a second opinion. She had to practically beg that doctor to check her child out because he didn't want to *step on the toes* of the other doctor. What is more important I ask you? He finally examined the child himself and determined that she had a rice cereal allergy. I often wondered what the first doctor would have told my friend, after finding her babies colon attached. Folks, we need doctors. But more importantly, we need to be our own doctors. We need to become proactive in our own health care. Doctors see hundreds of patients a year, but we know ourselves better than anyone else. Learn how to listen to your body and embrace symptoms as if your body is talking back to you. Don't cover symptoms with the Band-aid of over-the-counter and prescription drugs. Find the root cause and pull it out, or it will grow back.

About eight years ago, well into my new lifestyle, I had a bout of severe dizziness to the point of vomiting. My family and I had just returned from blackberry picking, and I thought maybe the berries were to blame. But no other family member felt the way I did. I hadn't been to the doctor in years, so I thought it would be good to get a checkup. With the knowledge I had acquired, I thought that I may have an iron deficiency. I can't do my own blood work so I made an appointment. As soon as I entered the examination room, the nurse took my vitals. I explained what I thought was wrong, and then she went to get the doctor.

The doctor walked in with prescription pad in hand. I retold the story to him and he wrote me a prescription for vertigo drugs. He said that it could have come from a middle-ear infection. I told him that I had absolutely no problem with my ears. I shared my idea of having low iron and asked if he could check it. He did and came back with the results of below average iron in my blood. He proceeded to write me another prescription for a coal tar form of iron pills and never took back the vertigo prescription. I had all that I needed from him. I went home, tore up the prescriptions and added more green barley grass powder and blackstrap molasses to my diet (both naturally high in iron). The dizziness never returned. Praise the Lord! You see, God's people are destroyed from a lack of knowledge (Hosea 4:6). I could have been taking vertigo pills without having vertigo and quite possibly suffering from some awful side-effects. We must be proactive with our health and that of our families.

"Bless the Lord, O my soul: and all that is within me, bless His holy name. Bless the Lord, O my soul, and forget not all His benefits: Who forgiveth all thine iniquities; who healeth all thy diseases; Who redeemeth thy life from destruction; Who crowneth thee with lovingkindness and tender mercies; Who satisfieth thy mouth with good things; so that thy youth is renewed like the eagle's" (Psalm 103:1-5 *KJV*). That last verse said that God's good things (good foods) satisfy, and our youth is renewed. It is safe to say the opposite must be true, that man's harmful/bad foods do not satisfy and make us feel old and sick.

If you've never heard this before, here it goes . . . What you eat *will* affect your health! We can see it all around us. Americans are getting heavier and in turn getting sicker. "Be not deceived; God is not mocked: for whatsoever a man soweth that shall he also reap" (Galatians 6:7 *KJV*). Whatever we sow, good or bad—healthy or unhealthy, that is what we'll reap. If this were not so, then why are thousands of folks changing their standard American diet and in turn reaping good health, strength and vitality? It's not rocket science. It is the simple "garbage in, garbage out" method. If you drop a watermelon from a ten-story building, it will smash onto the ground. Like gravity, our Creator has in place other natural laws. If you continue to fuel your body with man-made chemical-laden foods, your body will eventually get sick.

As Christians, we are promised life abundant here on earth (John 10:10). I'm not seeing it. The church is as sick as the world! Why is this, when by His stripes we are healed (Isaiah 53:5)? It is because we have conformed to the way the world eats, thinks and lives. "I Beseech you therefore, brethren, by the mercies of God, that ye present your bodies a living sacrifice, holy, acceptable unto God, which is your reasonable service. And be not conformed to this world; but be ye transformed by the renewing of your mind, that ye may prove what is that good, and acceptable, and perfect, will of God" (Romans 12:1-2 *KJV*).

Eating, drinking, thinking and living like the world is not good or acceptable. I share my experiences to help you renew your mind. Are you presenting your blood-bought body as a living sacrifice, holy and acceptable? Gluttony is not acceptable and being too busy to take care of your health is not reasonable. "Oh, but health foods are so expensive!" Well, it is not nearly as costly as a hospital stay. A non-believer may ask how we can share about a Savior who heals, when we have high cholesterol, high blood pressure and acid reflux. If your Jesus is so mighty, why hasn't He healed you? It is because, we have not separated ourselves from everything that contaminates and defiles both *body* and spirit, perfecting holiness in fear of God (2 Corinthians 6:7, 7:1).

The standard American diet contaminates and defiles your body, and in turn your body starts to break down and weaken. If your body could speak to you, it would *beg* you to fuel it with God-made nutritious foods, so that it runs properly. If you beat something up long enough, it will surrender and eventually die. "Do you not know that your body is the temple (the very sanctuary) of the Holy Spirit Who lives within you, Whom you have received (as a gift) from God? You are not your own, you were bought with a price (purchased with a preciousness and paid for, made His own). So then, honor God and bring glory to Him in your body" (1 Corinthians 6:19-20 *AMP*). This isn't legalism, this is worship. We worship Him when we take care of His holy temple. This one body is on loan to you; you are not your own. When a neighbor borrows something from you, you expect him to take good care of it. Right? God expects the same from us.

Do you know how wonderfully made you really are (Psalm 139:14)? Our bodies were created to be self-healing. If you break your leg the doctor may set it in a cast, but who weaves the bone back together? If you cut yourself, you may put a little ointment on the cut, but who forms the scab and new skin underneath? Our Creator designed us to self-correct but only if we do our part and supply the proper fuel required. The way Americans eat today is not the required fuel. Our lifestyle and diet has polluted our God-made bodies. Our bodies are drowning in these pollutants and we see sickness and disease on the rise. We are a nation that is overfed and under-nourished. We eat too much, and the quality of food is very low on the vitamin and mineral scale.

Let's look at self-pollution. Remember science class? We learned that we breathe in oxygen and breathe out carbon dioxide. Carbon dioxide is a waste product of our body, along with feces, urine and sweat. Man-made soda has a fizz that comes from carbon dioxide. The average American drinks soda almost every day. How can ingesting what our Creator has deemed waste, be good for us? We cannot continue to pour poisons down our throats (fungicides, herbicides, pesticides, preservatives, additives, chemicals, artificial colors and flavors etc.) without reaping some kind of negative effect.

The world does not care about us, because if it did, it wouldn't be tainting our food supply. Man cares about long shelf-life and the mighty dollar. I have saved thousands of dollars on doctors, over-the-counter drugs and prescriptions, simply because I have no need of them. That's where all of the extra money comes from to buy healthy food. Nowadays organic produce has come down considerably. I've often found organic produce cheaper than conventionally grown. So shop and compare before you buy.

I know someone who does care about us, God does! He wants everyone to have peace and balance of mind and body. Who better to tell us what to eat than the One who created us? Are you living the abundant life Christ died to give you? Are you doing your part in your relationship with Him? One-sided relationships never work out. Colossians 2:8 (*KJV*) tells us, "Beware lest any man spoil you through philosophy and vain deceit, after the tradition of men, after the rudiments of the world, and not after Christ." Who taught you how to cook, Mom? Who taught her how to cook? Grandma and her mother before her. The way we eat is a tradition of man. Yet we are passing this harmful lifestyle down to our children and grandchildren. It is time for someone in your family line to break the cycle. Could that special someone be you?

Most additives man has put into our foods have harmful effects. Did you know that the average American consumes over seven pounds of these toxins a year? When is it safe to consume chemicals? Often, I'll hear the response, "A little bit won't hurt you." Maybe not, but we don't eat a little bit! These poisons are in our breakfast, lunch, dinner, snacks, drinks, soap, shampoo, makeup, cleaners, carpets, environment . . . It is *not* a little bit! God did not make our bodies chemical and drug deficient. You may find it surprising that the word *pharmaceutical* comes from the Greek word *pharmakeia*, which means sorcery/witchcraft. Yikes! Chew on that one for a while.

God's original diet can be found in Genesis 1:29. It contained all fruits, vegetables, nuts, seeds, grains, beans and legumes. Meat was not included. Remember, there was no death before sin. The lion lay down with the lamb, and we were supposed to live forever (Isaiah 65:25). Many sources over the years have told us to limit our consumption of meat and increase our fruit and vegetable intake. Man has just found out what God knew all along. Animal foods have cholesterol and cholesterol clogs up our arteries. And that can lead to heart disease and stroke. God's original diet is cholesterol free! That's why when folks change their diet to God's diet, they reap better health. It's simple really. The church is as sick as the world simply because we have conformed to the ways of the world. Therefore, we suffer the same consequences. Which will you choose— man's way and sickness, or God's way with life abundant? Elijah asks in 1 Kings 18:21, "How long shall you be between two opinions? If the Lord be God, follow Him."

The biggest battle for me—and I believe most people—is the battle between my flesh and my spirit. The spirit man is the *real me*, the breath of life. My fleshy side has the sin nature at work inside me. So my carnal habitual nature will fight over these new healthy changes I want to implement.

This is the biggest battle, knowing the good to do and fighting myself to succeed.

As a believer, I know the devil is a defeated foe (Revelation 20:10). He only gets to do what I allow him to. My everyday enemy is myself. The battle is in my mind, trying to tell my flesh, *not* to desire the harmful things it is used to. Remember those old cartoons, where a man has a little angel on one shoulder and a little devil on the other? Each one whispers the right or wrong thing to do in his ear. That's like the flesh/spirit voices within us. Our spirit should be in constant communication with the Holy Spirit, Who teaches us what is best. Meanwhile, our carnal mind tries to talk us out of it. Therefore, when you start making healthy changes, the flesh will scream out, "Stop, you're killing me!" That's good! You are denying yourself, taking up your cross and following the Holy Spirit's voice (Mark 8:34). Romans 7:18-19 (*AMP*) says, "For I know that nothing good dwells within me, that is, in my flesh. I can will what is right, but cannot perform it. (I have the intention and urge to do what is right, but no power to carry it out.)For I fail to practice the good deeds I desire to do, but the evil deeds that I do not desire to do are what I am (ever) doing."

If you are ruled by your appetite and by what you think and feel, then you are ruled by your flesh. I had to learn to recognize who was speaking to me. I know I probably sound like I need to be in a strait-jacket, but I know you can relate. I want to liberate you. You will never win this battle until your breath leaves your body, so own it and learn how you operate. Learn what works and doesn't work for you. If harmful foods call to you from the pantry 24/7, don't keep any harmful food in your home. Why make it easy for the flesh to have the victory? Know yourself and know your weaknesses. Don't be a slave to your own flesh/carnal nature. Make your flesh a slave to you. Would you like to try a test to see how strong your flesh really is? Try fasting for a day and watch how your carnal side screams out. Yet, when you've beaten your flesh into submission, it is so empowering and such a high for your spirit (1 Corinthians 9:27). We often think of holiness as it pertains to the spiritual. But holiness is also in the physical.

1 Thessalonians 5:23 (*KJV*) says, "And the very God of peace sanctify you wholly: and I pray God your whole spirit and soul and body be preserved blameless unto the coming of our Lord Jesus Christ." So, the *body* is to be preserved blameless/holy also (1 Peter 1:16).

I never totally understood how we are tri-part beings, until I heard Joyce Meyer explain. She is such a practical teacher and I have learned much from her ministry. Our soul is our mind, will and emotions, which are part of our carnal nature. God's Word tells us that our body and mind are to be holy too, not just our spirit. Our bodies are the temple of the Holy Spirit. I have had a hard time wrapping my mind around that one. Scripture tells us we have received Christ as a gift from God. And the Holy Spirit has come to live within us. Thus, our bodies became the temple He now indwells (1 Corinthians 6:19-20). That is just too awesome for words! This verse has helped me tremendously over the years—helping me to make drastic changes in how I take care of my body, His holy temple.

The Reverend George Malkmus' book *Why Christians Get Sick*, helped me to see that I had to make dietary changes if I wanted to bring glory to God in my body. We need to be healthy representatives of Christ here on earth, so that we can be of service to Him as long as we can. Deuteronomy 30:19 (*AMP*) says, "I call heaven and earth to witness this day against you that I have set before you life and death, the blessings and the curses; therefore choose life, that you and your descendents may live." This warrants repeating. We must *choose* life and a healthy lifestyle so that our children and grandchildren may live!

We are passing down the standard American diet to our children and grandchildren. As a result, they are living with obesity, acid reflux and malnourished brains. It is time for us to begin anew and choose life-giving foods to pass down. Because I chose to change, I am reaping a wonderful life—and so are my children. As of this writing my daughters—sixteen and twenty—have never taken antibiotics. This is not to brag, but to prove these changes really do work. Moreover, I've never dealt with the terrible twos or teenage rebellion. Could it be that most children and teenagers today are so full of toxins and devoid of nutrients that their brains are starving? The standard American diet does not feed the cells of the brain properly so that— along with hormonal imbalance—our teens go through what I call, *the Dr Jekyll-Mr. Hyde syndrome.* Kids today are so pumped up on sugar, caffeine and a host of food additives that they don't know which end is up. They're pinging off the walls, moody and exhausted. I know my girls have inner peace because I feed them real God-made food.

Quite often, I read testimonies about how diet change has healed folks of cancer, ADD, PMS, migraines, diabetes, hypoglycemia . . . It isn't difficult really. All I did was read labels, eat *real* food, avoid animal products, get out doors in the fresh air and sunshine, exercise, drink purified water, add a few supplements that come from whole food sources, keep positive and pray for the Lord to guide me along the way. The humble person will seek help from the Lord and realize that he cannot do it alone. I can't. I tried it and it didn't work. You see, God did not leave us alone. On resurrection morning, the tomb was empty. He lives! He lives in you! He empowers you to do anything you need to do. Never forget Whose you are!

Often the Holy Spirit reminded me who I was *In Christ.* Philippians 2:13 (*AMP*) tells us, "For it is God Who is all the while effectually at work in you (energizing and creating in you the power and desire), both to will and to work for His good pleasure." If you are a follower of Christ, you already have the inner power to make the necessary changes. Scripture tells us that each of us should know how to control his own body (1 Thessalonians 4:4). I had to learn that the same Savior that bought my spirit back from hell is the same Savior that helps me with everyday struggles. He is not the one-time Savior; He is the every day, every moment Savior! Proverbs 14:12 (*AMP*) says, "There is a way which seems right to a man and appears straight before him, but at the end of it is the way of death." People think they are eating right, but they end up dying too soon. When I was a little girl, cancer was an old person's disease. Today, women in their early twenties are dying of breast cancer. I believe the Lord is asking us to raise our standard and come up higher.

This is how it works with the flesh/spirit battle . . . He that eats the most wins. I used to be spiritually anorexic and spiritually emaciated. I fed my flesh more and it became the stronger of the two. I had to do what Jeremiah did. He *ate* the Word and it was the joy and rejoicing of his heart (Jeremiah 15:16). The Word=Jesus=the Bread of Life! We must learn the Word because it is the only weapon that divides the soul and spirit (Hebrews 4:12). The Word tells us that when we walk in the spirit, we will not fulfill the desires of the flesh (Galatians 5:16). Make it a point to get fat on the Word every day. Supersize your portion of Bible reading and your spirit will crush the harmful habits of your carnal nature. Stay with Jesus until you're full, then there will be no room for the flesh to have its way. This is how we glorify God in our body. This is why I am living the abundant life Christ died to give me, here and now. I so want that for you as well.

Earlier, I mentioned that when the Lord initially taught me about nutrition, I learned the Levitical diet of clean and unclean foods. But the Lord took me farther back than Leviticus, to the very beginning in Genesis. Even now if I consume animal products, it is never unclean meats such as pork and shellfish. I may have turkey at a relative's home on Thanksgiving or Christmas but it is not the norm. This is how my family and I attain our healing testimonies. When my friend—who died from leukemia at 40—went on a raw diet for a short while, she shared with me the source of her information; a ministry called Hallelujah Acres. Reverend George Malkmus started the ministry after receiving healing in his body from colon cancer.

After purchasing their literature, I began the second phase of my journey. I continued studying and researching. Then in 2002 I went to their headquarters to earn my certification to become a Health Minister. Part of my ministry is teaching the Hallelujah diet—which consists of mostly raw food. Thousands of people all over the world have received healing in their body by incorporating this diet into their lives. Check out their website www.hacres.com and read the miraculous encouraging testimonies. I realize that my journey will never be over, until the Lord calls me home. I am always open to learning about new ways to improve the quality of life. So, the journey continues . . .

ACIDIC OR ALKALINE

In all my years of learning about nutrition, calorie counting, weighing food, portion control, carbohydrate counting, omitting fat and fad diets, I was always brought back to one thing—get alkaline and get healthy. Surprisingly, I found that cancer cells start to die with a pH level of 8.0. They die in an alkaline body! God's original diet—when we were supposed to live forever—is an alkaline diet. Common sense tells us that if cancer cells die, then other diseases may die as well. So our goal should not be carb and calorie counting. Instead, our goal should be consuming foods that make us alkaline, and staying away from foods that make us acidic. The weight loss and energy increase will simply follow an alkaline diet and stress-free lifestyle.

Raw foods are living foods. Living foods contain enzymes. Every function of the human body requires enzymes. Yet only raw, living foods contain these vital enzymes. Enzyme rich foods include raw fruits, raw vegetables, raw unsalted unroasted nuts and seeds, raw sprouted grains, seeds and legumes. If we heat our food over 107°, the enzymes will be destroyed. A dear friend blessed me with a dehydrator that has a thermostat control that *cooks* food at low temperatures without destroying the living enzymes. I have made things like fruit leather, banana chips and even almond milk yogurt in my dehydrator without sacrificing those precious enzymes to high heat. You can eat hot oatmeal for breakfast, almond butter and jelly on whole wheat bread for lunch and whole wheat pasta with tomato sauce for dinner—and these are all great. But, you would not have consumed one living enzyme.

The key to getting healthy is getting alkaline. The key to getting alkaline is making a large percent of your diet raw, living foods. When I consume living foods I feel more satisfied and I eat less. My appetite is normal and I don't have the desire to overeat. Our Creator has placed in each of us what I like to call the *hunger switch*. When the body has been given foods that satisfy its nutritional needs, the switch turns off. That's why after I've eaten chips, soda and cake I still feel hungry afterward. The hunger switch will not turn off until the cells have been satisfied with the nutrients it requires.

The opposite of an alkaline body is an acidic body. An acidic body is more prone to sickness and disease. Foods that come from animal sources, man-made processed foods, hydrogenated oils and sugar rich foods are probably the most acidic to the body. There is an awesome booklet called, *The China Project* by T. Colin Campbell PH.D and Christine Cox. It has made a huge impact on me concerning foods from animal sources. The booklet helped me to understand what these foods do to my body—and it isn't pretty. The standard American diet is a mostly acidic diet.

The easiest way to consume raw living food is to invest in a vegetable juicer. With a juicer I was able to ingest larger amounts of raw fruits and vegetables. For example, I would juice one pound of carrots, which filled an eight-ounce glass with juice. It sure is easier to drink the eight ounces of carrot juice than to chomp on one pound of raw carrots. The juice is surprisingly sweet and refreshing. I'd use carrot as my base and then add all kinds of other veggies I had on hand in smaller quantities. I would often add raw garlic to the juice. Now that's a kick in the taste buds! Blending raw fruit and vegetable smoothies is another way of consuming large amounts of enzyme rich foods.

Simply put, 3 things cause sickness:

- *Toxicity*. Too many poisons breathed, absorbed and ingested

- *Deficiency*. Not enough nutrient rich foods consumed

- *Stress*. Stress is like a cork on your big toe that pops off and all of the healthy nutrients you consumed spill out, as though you never ingested them. Stress stops up our organs so horribly that they'll hold onto toxins instead of removing them. The enzyme rich juices quickly absorb into our bodies helping to melt away stress. I have experienced for myself the life-giving benefits of keeping my body alkaline and it hasn't failed me yet.

Being alkaline keeps us healthy. We are all subject to germs and disease. The difference is whether my body is the perfect environment for the germ or virus. If my body is stressed out and acidic, and I come in contact with a flu bug, my body will gladly host the germ or virus and make it welcome. However, if the same bug came in contact with a stress-free alkaline body, it would have no safe place to land. My strong immune system would destroy it before it had the chance. I know folks who have not had a cold in years because of their raw eating and stress-free living.

THE FORGOTTEN SIN

In all of my years of following Jesus I have yet to hear a message on gluttony. The Bible lumps the glutton together with the drunkard in Proverbs 23:21 and Deuteronomy 21:20.

Is food your god? Do you run to food for comfort, peace, rest, pleasure, security or companionship? Are you dealing with emotional troubles in the physical? By now I hope that you can see that it doesn't work; at least it never has for me. Once you've eaten to sustain life, you need to allow the Spirit of the Lord to produce self control in your life. There is no need to continually pray for it, just spend time with Him. The fruit of the Spirit is the result of spending time with the Holy Spirit.

Beware of eating unconsciously. I used to sit in front of the TV with a big bowl of popcorn and become so engrossed in the movie, I didn't even realize that I had eaten the whole thing in a matter of minutes. Take control of what's controlling you. Learn how you operate so that you can guard against unhealthy habits. You must expect the flesh to suffer hunger, in order to reverse gluttonous behavior. When we deal with emotional things spiritually, we have the Holy Satisfier who supernaturally helps us to crucify our carnal desires daily (Galatians 5:24).

"O God, You are my God, earnestly will I seek You; my inner self thirsts for You, my flesh longs and is faint for You, in a dry and weary land where no water is. My whole being shall be satisfied as with marrow and fatness; and my mouth shall praise You with joyful lips" (Psalm 63:1, 5 *AMP*). Do brownies, potato chips or soda satisfy your *whole* being? In a nation that is growing heavier on harmful foods, Christ intended us to get fat on Him! Nothing else can satisfy like Jesus. Habitually, we reach for food when we actually may be thirsty for water. Often, we try to satisfy the flesh with food and drink when our spirits are hungry. Instead of pizza, we should praise Him. Instead of potato chips . . . praise. Praise away the cravings for harmful foods. Try it; you can actually turn your mind away from overeating, by simply stopping to praise the Lord! There is power in praise! Pop in a CD, sing a happy tune unto Jesus and watch Him satisfy you with spiritual fatness.

I often hear people say, "Depression makes me overeat." I admit the daily routine can become monotonous. But I wonder if you might be confusing depression with plain old boredom. You may need your own mini-adventure to get rejuvenated again. Find an adventure that doesn't conflict with your responsibilities and go for it! Something as simple as eating outdoors during your lunch hour can put a little spring into your step, not to mention getting some *real air* into your lungs. Taking a sunset stroll after dinner can be relaxing and a great way to change up the daily routine.

Romans 12:1-2 tells us to renew our minds, which helps us not to conform to the ways of the world. It is my prayer that you will change your old thought process, to a new and healthier one. We all have experienced poor health at one time or another; it's no picnic. It hinders our lives on so many levels. Americans today *live to eat.* We need to think of our food as something that sustains quality of life, not merely an act that temporarily brings pleasure to our taste buds. Ask yourself, *Am I really in control of my appetite?* Unrestrained bad habits of any kind, can be life threatening.

It is always the right time to do the right thing. Go to the Word for your medicine. Run to the Savior, not junk food, to satisfy you. Jesus will be the answer to your cravings, if you allow Him. He is your antidepressant, appetite suppressant, joy and strength. Discover how you can *eat to live* and enjoy the bounty of God's goodness.

"So, brethren, we (who are born again) are not children of a slave woman (the natural), but of the free (the supernatural). In (this) freedom Christ has made us free (and completely liberated us); stand fast then and do not be hampered and held ensnared and submit again to a yolk of slavery (which you have once put off)" (Galatians 4:31-5:1 *AMP*).

BALANCE

Are you at church or work so often that you don't know the name of your child's best friend? What is your wife's favorite color? What is your husband's favorite sports team? Are you missing it? Are you missing out on your life? Imagine for a moment that you have every *thing* that you have ever wanted; a large home, sports car, loads of money in the bank, a high paying job, boat, motorcycle, designer clothes, jewelry . . . Bask in that for a moment or two. Now, take every human being off the face of the earth, it's just you and your *things.* Reflect on that for a while. Suddenly, all of your *stuff* becomes meaningless. Without relationships with other people, life is pretty empty. Take a look at the time you spend with those *things.* How do they rob you of your relationship with others?

I've been a substitute teacher for years, from K-5—12th grade in Christian schools. I heard a lot of stories from students. Often they'd talk to me about things they'd never tell their parents. I recall chatting with four or five senior girls. I told them my girls wanted to marry their dad when they were little. He was their boyfriend, to hug and to kiss. I asked those high school girls if they had felt that way about their fathers. They all gazed at me as if I were from another planet. I'm sure my countenance fell because I could feel my heart sinking. I wondered how that could be. They were Christian girls with godly fathers. Yet one girl said her dad hardly spoke to her. Another said she was closer to her mom. And still another said her dad never had time for her. I'm sure these dads provided well for their girls; they were in a private Christian school for goodness sake. Yet these dads missed it and, in turn, the girls missed out as well.

Dads, you need to date your daughters! You are the first example of Christ in your child's life. How you treat them is what they will typically look for in a husband. Balance is kicking the ball around with them when all you really want to do is watch TV. Balance is showing up for their soccer game by cancelling your golf game. We only have our children for a short time. Golf will always be there, but they won't. Children are on loan for us to love, value, empower, and to give purpose and direction. We are to train them in the ways of the Lord. Then we can set them free to do the same.

Early in my marriage, my husband used to play on the computer so often, that I called it *the other woman*. Balance is shutting the computer off when your wife comes over to hug your neck—not continuing to play over her shoulder. Wives, if you're out with your girlfriends more than with your man, you are out-of-balance. When your spouse needs your attention and affection, be sure to accommodate him. Ladies, we tend to multi-task and burn ourselves out. Stop putting so much on your plate and learn to say no. Repeat after me . . . "No"! See, that wasn't so hard. "Oh by the way, could you help me with Sunday school, Vacation Bible School, children's church, ladies' Bible study, pot luck, coffee hour, food bank, cleaning pews, homeless shelter . . . ?" Balance is saying, "I appreciate your asking but I already have too much on my plate." When your plate becomes less full, you can offer your services again. Believe me, the ones asking will find someone else to do it. I wonder if some folks never get called on to help because the same ten people are doing everything. There are many parts to the body and they *all* need to be involved.

I have a friend whose husband is jealous of her Jesus. He doesn't like for her to do much without him. My friend would love for her husband to join her at church and other Christian functions. But he won't have any part of it, insisting he is a Christian. He feels his wife needs him less when she goes off to Bible study and weekday services. She has even given up some of her functions to stay at home to be with him. His pride keeps him from enjoying who she is in Christ. It keeps him from knowing and enjoying Jesus for himself. She has prayed many years for her out-of-balance husband to join her (1 Peter 3:1-5). He needs his own personal walk with his Savior. Deep down I think he wants that too.

When your spouse has finished a long day at work, does he dread coming home? Will he be bombarded at the door with a myriad of complaints? You may have legitimate cause to complain but wait until the man peels off his dirty work clothes, washes his face and eats his meal. Then you can have a *peaceful* discussion. Make your house the kind of place he longs to come home to. Strive to make it a place of peace, rest, nourishment and love.

When I became a new mom, I wanted to be the perfect wife and mother. The house would be clean, laundry done and baby fed and happy at all times. Of course, dinner would be ready as soon as my husband walked through the door. I remember feeling guilty (as a stay-at-home mom) if my husband helped me with the domestic chores. I felt as if I'd failed at my job because he already worked all day. But keeping up with this routine made me nuts! Not to mention I was only working with a few hours of sleep. Who was I kidding? After a while of trying desperately to keep up my *super woman* pace, I'd break down. This often included lashing out at my husband. I am not *Superwoman,* and I don't have an "*S*" on my chest. You are not *Superwoman,* nor will you ever be.

Who cares if there are dishes in the sink and your husband has to make himself a sandwich when he gets home? It's okay, and it won't make you any less of a wife or mother. Liberate yourself, and do what you can. What you don't do will still be there, until you get to it. Dads, balance is letting your wife run to the grocery store while you care for Junior. Caring for him while she showers and pampers herself a bit will bless you more than it will her, believe me. She will feel better and in turn you will have a pleasant woman to be around. This early stage lasts just a season, and together you will get through it.

Ladies, do you realize the power you have as wives and moms? On occasion I have literally brought the whole house down by myself. I proved this over many a meal, when my girls were young. Everyone was happy and enjoying pleasant conversation, but for some silly reason I was irritable. I complained about petty things that should have been overlooked. I could sense in my spirit that I was headed down the wrong road; I needed to detour. Yet I disobeyed the Holy Spirit's prompting to keep my mouth shut. Instantly my girls started pouting and my husband shot me a look. He also sided with them, which angered me all the more. I succeeded in changing the entire mood of my house from calm to cantankerous—resulting in disrupted digestion and mental anguish. Later, I always felt awful.

Over the years I've learned one of my hardest lessons—how to keep my mouth closed. Everything that drops into my mind does not have to come out of my mouth. The evidence of self-control is a fitly spoken word, a timely word, an encouraging word (Isaiah 50:4, Proverbs 25:11). The destructive words that rob a home of peace are contrary to a Christ-like behavior. Jesus warned that on the day of judgment we will have to give an account for every idle word we speak (Matthew 12:36). As I learned this lesson early on, I realized I didn't have much to say. Keeping quiet was a healing transition that my flesh had to learn and form a new habit doing. Now when harmful thoughts enter my mind I am in control. I choose to flick them out so that they cannot spill out of my mouth (Ephesians 4:29-32). It is empowering to say the least. My spirit cheers inside because of the victory over my flesh. Hallelujah!

Through all my tests and trials I am becoming a Proverbs 31 woman. This virtuous woman is called to trust and honor her husband as the leader of the home. She desires to raise her children according to the word of God. She is a diligent keeper of the home and knows that motherhood is a price-less profession. She is wise with the time and money the Lord entrusts to her. She is spiritually, mentally and physically prepared for the tasks that lie before her. Her home is a safe and welcome environment. She opens her mouth with kindness, good judgment and sound advice. She is not selfish or idle and offers help to those in need. She has strength of character and her family thinks she's the greatest. So you see we are called to be part of the solution not part of the problem.

Along those same lines, we need to address criticism. Criticizing your spouse will destroy intimacy, affection and romance in your marriage.

Criticizing your children will close up their spirits. As a result, they will build walls to defend their hearts from the pain. I have yet to meet a critic with balance. Embrace the power you have in your words. Recognize when you are using them to build up or tear down. Healing only comes when you admit you have a problem. Then surrender to the Holy Spirit's conviction and obey what He prompts you to do to correct it.

Being in debt is not conducive to a balanced life. In fact, it is quite the opposite. Debt damages relationships, and God does not advocate it (Romans 13:8). Debt is a self-inflicted burden that has hurt and even destroyed many marriages/relationships. Money is not evil, but the love of money—yearning for, attachment to, adoration of—it is (1 Timothy 6:10). Money is a good thing; it buys clothes, food and shelter—things we need. Moreover, it allows us to bless the less fortunate. The *love* of money goes beyond *need* to *want, covetousness and greed*. Money can be a very powerful persuasion. My husband has often said, "I'm not trying to keep up with the Joneses; I'm trying to keep away from them." Over the past decade the average person has been working hard to keep up with the Hollywood elite. Everyone wants to be a diva. Everyone wants to wear designer *this* and brand name *that*. Those stars are making millions! We shouldn't even try to keep up with them.

I recall a Saturday morning when my young daughters were watching cartoons. Suddenly a commercial for a scantily clothed doll burst onto the screen. She wore all the bling and fashion that Hollywood could drum up. The advertisement, geared toward four to eight-year-old girls, used words and phrases that really disturbed me—"be a superstar, fashion model, diamonds, furs, rich and famous." It was disgusting to watch. No wonder young girls are dressing and acting like they're twenty-five. To make matters worse, moms encourage this behavior because they're caught up in it as well. Women often put their families in hock by trying to live like Hollywood stars. Sadly, they are teaching their children by example. These women—and often men—attempt to fund a lifestyle the family can't afford. Imagine the stress put on family finances.

You don't need to buy the latest and greatest item on the market. If what you have still works, you don't need to buy a new one. I've told my girls for years, "Mom and Dad will buy you what you need, and you can buy the things you want." As soon as they figured out that meant spending their own money, the item wasn't as appealing. They wanted it more when we paid for it. This responsibility helped them respect what they had. Moreover, they saved more and spent less. Today, they are both good stewards of their money. "Train up a child in the way he should go: and when he is old, he will not depart from it" (Proverbs 22:6 *KJV*).

Balance tells us to spend less and enjoy a simpler life because simplicity begets peace. I am a happy princess, not because we have millions, but because we are debt free. I believe this is one of many reasons why our marriage is both healthy and successful. My husband and I are happy and content. The power of balance and simplicity really works, I challenge you to try it (Matthew 6:19-24). It is so liberating!

WHOSE YOU ARE

Does your mind get you into trouble? You're sitting there minding your own business when something calls to you from inside the pantry, "Come and eat me." It calls out until you get up off your chair and give in to whatever it is. The same thing happens in the grocery store. That's why we shouldn't go shopping on an empty stomach. Don't you hate it when inanimate objects have power over you? I liken it to the slapstick comedy of a man trying to retrieve his hat while continually kicking it away. Recognize what you are doing to yourself. Why keep your pantry loaded with harmful foods that continue to call to you when you really don't want to consume them? Whose side are you on anyway? It's time to be on your own side and get the garbage out of your home! If you are like me, you will eat it if it's there. If the cookies, chips and candy are not in the house, then you can't eat them. That includes your private stash and you know who you are.

Parents often tell me they keep that kind of food around for the kids. If it is unhealthy for you, then obviously it's unhealthy for them. The power of a parents influence on a child is great. If you live the healthy example, they will respect what you say. It is time to throw away the ol', *"Do as I say, not as I do"* philosophy. It doesn't work. In fact, it is detrimental to all relationships. We all know that you are only as good as your word. The power of choice is everything. Your mother chose not to abort you; you chose to get married; you chose to have sex; you chose to get pregnant. All of life is choices, good or bad, helpful or hurtful. Twenty years ago I chose to delve into nutrition. That was a good choice. Thank you Lord!

"I appeal to you therefore, brethren, and beg of you in view of (all) the mercies of God, to make a decisive dedication of your bodies (presenting all your members and faculties) as a living sacrifice, holy (devoted, consecrated) and well pleasing to God, which is your reasonable (rational, intelligent) service and spiritual worship. Do not be conformed to this world (this age), (fashioned after and adapted to its external, superficial customs), but be transformed (changed) by the (entire) renewal of your mind (by its new ideals and its new attitude), so that you may prove (for yourselves) what is the good and acceptable and perfect will of God, even the thing which is good and acceptable and perfect (in His sight for you)" (Romans 12:1-2 *AMP*). So how do we do this mind-renewing thing? We can start by heeding what the Word says. "A man's (moral) self shall be filled with the fruit of his mouth; and with the consequences of his words he must be satisfied (whether good or evil)" (Proverbs 18:20 *AMP*).

Growing up, I always saw the glass as half-empty, not half-full. As a child I hated to participate in things where I couldn't succeed. I was bossy, stubborn and always wanted to be right. Over the years I learned, that to truly be right, you must admit when you're wrong. Praise was rare at my house and I built walls to defend myself from emotional and physical pain. It's true that, *you are what you eat*. It is also true that, *you are what you think*. We will live by the consequences of our negative thoughts, *if* those thoughts spill out of our mouths.

How do you talk to yourself? At times our *self-talk* is destructive. We wouldn't even talk to our enemies the way we talk to ourselves. Scripture tells us that we will live with the consequences of our words toward ourselves and others. Positive words equal positive results, and negative words, negative results. We need to line up our thoughts/words with those of our Creator and how he sees us. If I tell myself that I am a stupid, boring, loser, then who am I agreeing with? I know the Bible doesn't say that about me. So I can choose to entertain the father of lies, or believe the truth of God's holy Word. It is the truth that sets us free (John 8:32). Lies keep us in bondage.

Complaining, rooted in pride, slowly chisels away at the receiver's self-worth. The complainer usually can dish it out, but acts indignant if she is on the receiving end. I was a complainer. Since I didn't become conscious of this for a long time, I wasted precious time doing it. Regretfully, I have reaped the consequences of my negative words. Honestly, you'd never speak again if you did not share some negative stories or situations that may have occurred. But I'm talking about the folks who find something wrong with most everything and feel compelled to enlighten everyone around. Complainers have a tough time looking inward to find faults to correct; it's usually always someone else who has the problem. Often it isn't obvious to the complainer that they are being destructive. Only the Holy Spirit can help them to make changes *if* they heed His promptings. We are told to do all things without grumbling and complaining (Philippians 2:14). I have come to realize that when we find fault in relation to how God created someone, in whatever area, we are disrespecting our Divine Designer. If you are jealous of the soloist at church, the friend at work or a family member, then you really don't know who *you* are in Christ. Comparison destroys contentment. When I truly learned who I was in Christ, I celebrated other's gifts and talents. Each one of us is created as valuable to God for a divine and distinctive purpose.

"Your life is a journey you must travel with a deep consciousness of God. It cost God plenty to get you out of that dead-end, empty-headed life you grew up in. He paid with Christ's sacred blood, you know. He died like an unblemished, sacrificial lamb. Even though it has only lately–at the end of the ages–become public knowledge, God always knew He was going to do this for you. It's because of this sacrificed Messiah, whom God then raised from the dead and glorified, that you trust God, that you know you have a future in God" (1 Peter 1:18-21 *The Message Bible*). You were worth dying for (Matthew 18:12-14). In view of the fact that you are that important to God, you must learn fully of His unconditional love for you. When I finally lined up my thoughts and words with who God said I was, the healing (renewing) of my mind started to take place. We need to continually remind ourselves who we are and Whose we are.

Let's take a closer look at who you are in Christ. Your mind may tell you that you are nobody, but you are a child of God (Romans 8:16). Individuals may say that you will never have the victory, but you are redeemed from the hand of the enemy (Psalms 107:2). Your old friends will never let you forget your past and you fear you will never be forgiven. Your Creator says that you are justified (just as if you'd never done it) by faith (Romans 5:1). You may *feel* like you are worthless and filthy, but your Savior says you are a new creature in Christ and you are sanctified (to be pure from sin/holy) (2 Corinthians 5:17). You may assume that you will never achieve anything worthwhile but your Lord says you are a partaker of His divine nature (2 Peter 1:4).

Do you believe that your family heritage has left you accursed? Well, your Savior has purchased your freedom from the curse of the law (Galatians 3:13). Hallelujah! All curses are broken. Our Redeemer lives! We serve a living God, and all other religions serve dead gods. Up until now, dark clouds always seemed to follow you and you felt like your life was jinxed. Yet your Heavenly Father says you are delivered from the controls and powers of darkness (Colossians 1:13). As a child of God you are never alone. You are never left without a guide (Romans 8:14). Do you live in fear of your safety? Is your *self talk* telling you that something terrible is going to happen to you or your family? The Lord our refuge tells us His angels will accompany, defend and preserve us in all of our ways (Psalm 91:11). Fear is not from God; fear is from the enemy. Who do you agree with? Faith is the opposite of fear. Whatever is not faith, is sin (Romans 14:23).

There is a vast difference between needs and wants. If you take a hard look at your needs, you will find that Christ has fulfilled them all and will continue to do so as He has promised (Philippians 4:19). As earthly fathers care for their children, your heavenly Father cares for you, except He loves and cares for you like no one else can. I grew up without an earthly father. But Jesus has filled that void to the full and overflowing. I know He will never disappoint, reject or leave me. No earthly love can ever compare to His unconditional love. When my heart is hurting, I can literally feel His warm soothing presence filling me with Fatherly care and concern. He is my mighty Sovereign God whom I fear, but He is also my comforting

Daddy who rocks away all my pain and sorrow. Our Creator is so neat that way. What other god does that?

We renew our minds by choosing to form new habits in our flesh. You once told yourself negative things. Now that you know that you are agreeing with the devil when you say those things; stop! Stop and quote scripture that exclaims who you *really* are. Begin by literally taking God at His word. When you are anxious or edgy and your mind has no peace, remember what Jehovah Shalom said. Throw those cares, worries and concerns once and for all on me and I will take care of it all for you (1 Peter 5:7). When I truly learned how to do this, I was profoundly liberated. Often I've heard others say, "Just lay your cares at the foot of the cross." Well, I tried that. But by the end of my prayer, I bent down and scooped them right back up again. I realized I didn't really trust Jesus with my problems. What was I thinking? The world Creator, star Breather and the risen Savior couldn't take care of my concerns? Later I realized I had difficulty relinquishing control. Hey, my mom *wore the pants* in the family my whole life. She brought home the bacon and took care of the household with all that it entailed. Mom was a strong-willed, independent, stubborn woman. So I learned from the best. My sisters and I refer to this ingrained way of thinking, as *mommy-itis*. Since we all had it, we all had to go through many trials and painful prunings to learn that it wasn't healthy.

We are all products of our upbringing. As a child we had no choice but to go with the flow–the good, the bad and the ugly. As adults however, we can choose to continue the harmful legacy or choose a different path. We have no more excuses. On my own I couldn't battle the *mommy-itis*, but I chose to change one baby step at a time. I knew I could draw my strength from Christ. He would empower me to change. Our union with Christ is a supernatural combination–He's super and we're natural. We're an unstoppable team! I'd be lying to you if I told you that the *mommy-itis* stayed dead in the grave. I'm by no means perfect, but I am happily on the other side. I no longer allow my past to control me. Yahoo! I can do *all* things through Christ who gives me strength (Philippians 4:13). Webster's says that *all* means the whole, everything, wholly and entirely. Now that's empowering to say the least!

Please try to grasp the supernatural power available to you in the Holy Spirit. Who are you in Christ? You are His! You are an heir to the blessings of Abraham (Galatians 3:14). You are an heir to eternal life (1 John 5:11-12). You are blessed coming in and going out (Deuteronomy 28:6). You are blessed with *all* (there's that word again) spiritual blessings (Ephesians 1:3). You are above and not beneath (Deuteronomy 28:13), more than a conqueror (Romans 8:37), and a laborer together with God (1 Corinthians 3:9). Wow, with Jesus we've got everything, so why do *life* alone? Why listen to the voice of the lower nature (flesh), when it is contrary to our Messiah's voice? It's easier said than done, I know. I would typically take two steps forward and one step back. The problem is we're only human.

Can I liberate you for a moment? You will never stop making mistakes, and you will never *not* need Jesus. God will never force Himself on you, and you will never lose the freedom to mess up. But, the same Jesus who saved you from sin, death and hell saves you from everyday mistakes. He is your everyday Savior, not just that one time. We are walking out our salvation one day at a time (Philippians 2:12). Freedom! Free to try our best, possibly mess up, repent, dust ourselves off and start fresh the very next moment. Born again! Jesus Christ is your personal Savior, partner and forgiver. He is on your side. Nothing you've done or will ever do will catch Him off guard or surprise Him. He knows the end from the beginning (Isaiah 46:10). Yippy! I now understand what Paul meant in becoming a fool for Christ (1 Corinthians 4:10). It is a blissful freedom, wrapped in an awesome unconditional love that no one can ever take from me. Sweet surrender . . . Thank you Lord!

So how did I get to that point? How did I keep those destructive, unhealthy thoughts from taking root? Faith and prayer are a powerful team. I knew the Word told me not to be moved by what I see (2 Corinthians 4:18). So I prayed for spiritual understanding. I needed eyes to see situations and circumstance the way Christ saw them. Every day I prayed with my *heavenly glasses*. Looking at the *big picture*–instead of the one right in front of me–taught me how to walk by faith and not by sight (2 Corinthians 5:7). Then, I had to learn to corral negative thoughts that dropped into my head or that someone else spoke. The following verse was the all-powerful key in obtaining my victory: "Inasmuch as we refute arguments *and* theories *and* reasonings and every proud and lofty thing that sets itself up against the (true) knowledge of God; and we lead every thought *and* purpose away captive into the obedience of Christ (the Messiah, the Anointed One)" (2 Corinthians 10:5 *AMP*). In other words, every wrong thought in my mind was taken away captive (made a prisoner, kept in bondage or ensnared) and was replaced by what God said about the circumstance. I repeated that verse over and over . . . "I take every thought captive into the obedience of Christ." Those word curses in my mind (the combat zone), *had* to obey God's Word! I continued to exercise my authority over the enemy by establishing His Word here on earth (Luke 10:19; Matthew 16:19). Negative thoughts left my mind and Christ's peace poured down over me like warm honey. It's time for the body of Christ to tap into the power we have as children of God, by truly knowing *Whose* we are (Galatians 3:26).

35

Guess What? You're Gifted!

Why are you *bent* a certain way? He loves to take the leadership role in tasks and projects. She jumps at the chance to help out when there is a need. We are all created with different spiritual gifts. It's what makes us who we are as individuals. When God created you, He did it for a reason and for a purpose. You are so very valuable to Him and to His divine plan. Knowing what your spiritual gifts are will help you find out what your natural area of ministry is.

Those gifts are evangelism, perceiver, teacher, exhorter, pastor, mercy, server, giver, healer and administrator (Romans 12:4-8; Ephesians 4:10-12; 1 Corinthians 12). Spiritual gifts are the main channel the Holy Spirit uses to guide the believer, in service to God. Yet each of our gifts is only a part of the body; together we are whole and fully functional. That's why we need one another; no one part is any more important than the other. Utilizing your gift brings inner joy and a warm sense of belonging. "As each of you has received a gift (a particular spiritual talent, a gracious divine endowment), employ it for one another as (befits) good trustees of God's many-sided grace (faithful stewards of the extremely diverse powers and gifts granted to Christians by unmerited favor)" (1 Peter 4:10 *AMP*). The Lord gifts each of us and we serve Him through those gifts. Where He guides, He provides and empowers us to complete each task for His glory and our self-worth.

Learning my gifts and those of my family has truly helped our relationships. Understanding how we're each *wired* has taught us patience and empowered us to embrace individual strengths. Learning my children's gifts has helped me to steer them away from their weaknesses and focus on their God-given abilities. Educating a pre-teen in his area of giftedness celebrates who he is at a questioning time in his life.

All we really want in this life is to be loved and needed. Showing your loved ones their value through their God-given gifts empowers them with purpose. You really can't go wrong. Since your Creator has equipped you with certain talents, you are guaranteed success, and there is no better boss to serve. He is loving, kind, slow to anger, patient and knows all your weaknesses. He wants you to be successful and coaches you along each step of the way. This is a win-win situation. God is not partial; not any one person is more important to him than another and each gift is equally important to Him (Acts 10:34).

I encourage you to study each area of giftedness and learn how you're *bent*. There are quite a few books written on the Spiritual gifts, which makes it easy to determine what yours may be. Once you have an idea, put it to the test by getting involved in your church. If you are a teacher, for example, adult Sunday school may be the place to start. If you are uncomfortable there, then go on to another area, maybe teaching children is more to your liking. It will take some time to figure out, so keep plugging away. You will have an inner knowing/peace confirming that you are in the right place. Once we understand our own gifts, we can accept and encourage each other's place within the body. The feeling of purpose and value is a spiritual high like no other. Moreover, you need never retire from this position (your service to God). Exercise your area of giftedness and find true contentment and joy.

WIELD YOUR SWORD

As many of you know, the armor of God is described in Ephesians 6:10-20. Over the years I often heard about the belt of truth, the breastplate of righteousness, the shoes of peace, the shied of faith, the helmet of salvation and the sword (which is the Word of God). Each piece protects us from the blows of the enemy, but the sword is our only offensive weapon. They are all vitally important, but without the sword, we'd just be standing there. It is time for us to fight back. Jesus used the sword when He was tempted by the devil in the wilderness (Matthew 4:1-11). He had fasted forty days and forty nights and was very hungry. Isn't it just like the enemy to start bugging us when we're not quite ourselves? But every time he bombarded Jesus with lies and accusations Jesus came back with the sword, the Word of God. He simply said, "It is written" . . .

I have a dear Peruvian friend, who often told me to pray the Word. She shared with me how powerful praying the Word was and how it had changed her life. I thought I was already doing that, but after listening to what the Lord had taught her, I realized I had only scratched the surface. Often I used the Word to see what was wrong with everyone else but myself. It took a while for the Holy Spirit to break through my arrogance, but thank God He never gave up on me. I have since learned to wield my sword successfully by faith. It truly is supernatural, and every believer is sadly missing out by not grasping the awesome power of speaking God's Holy Word aloud. After all, Jesus *is* the Word (John 1:1, Revelation 19:13). "So shall my word be that goes forth out of My mouth: it shall not return to Me void (without producing any effect, useless), but it shall accomplish that which I please and purpose, and it shall prosper in the thing for which I sent it" (Isaiah 55:11 *AMP)*. Okay, that sounds like another winner to me!

I wanted to experience all that Christ had for me, so I asked the Holy Spirit to teach me how to use my sword effectively. The old me would tense up and become fearful when a difficult situation suddenly arose. I was taught that F.E.A.R is *"False Evidence Appearing Real."* The enemy uses it to trick us into losing our faith. There is no fear in love; but perfect love casts out fear (1 John 4:18). The truth is, if you are always in fear, then you do not know how much God loves you. God is that perfect love and if you truly knew that in the depths of your heart, you would not live in fear or torment (1 John 4:7, 8). Make the time to study the love of God, and the fear will be expelled from your life.

Speaking the Word over my life did two things for me. It sent the enemy running in the opposite direction, and it built my faith by allowing my own ears to hear it. Yes, I talk to myself. I tell my flesh who is boss. It works in the natural and the spiritual realm because faith comes when we *hear* the Word of God (Romans 10:17). Again, our spirit needs to be in constant communication with the Holy Spirit in order to discern what His will is. It is not always clear but where the Prince of Peace guides, He provides His peace. "Forever, O Lord, thy word is settled in heaven" (Psalm 119:89 *KJV*). "Heaven and earth shall pass away, but my words shall not pass away" (Matthew 24:35 *KJV*). Scripture clearly tells us that the Word of the Lord endures forever; it is permanent (1 Peter 1:25). So how is His will done on earth as it is in heaven (Matthew 6:9-10)? We establish it on earth every time we speak it. "My son, attend to my words; consent and submit to my sayings. Let them not depart from your sight; keep them in the center of your heart. For they are life to those who find them, *healing* and *health* to all of their flesh" (Proverbs 4:20-22 *AMP*). This clearly tells us that our spiritual walk affects our physical health and well-being. We cannot have good health in our mind/body and the abundant life promised without submitting to His Holy Word. Simply put, obedience equals life abundant.

I learned how to use my sword by putting it to the test. When a potential problem or concern came my way, I paused straightway and asked the Holy Spirit to direct me. I then listened to the situation and calmly retrieved my book of promises. (You'll find this book at any Christian book store with scripture categorized under titles like *help, healing, protection, peace*). I went into my bedroom alone to speak God's Word aloud over the situation. One instance in particular concerned my teenage daughter. I was uncomfortable with what she was telling me. But I refused to allow the enemy to rob me of my peace, so I retreated to my quiet place to pray the Word aloud. Just like Jesus in the wilderness, I prayed the scripture that applied to the situation at hand. Such a sweet peace enveloped me as I cast my cares upon my Heavenly Father. You see, since Jesus is alive and Jesus is the Word, the Word is alive! It lives and breathes and has power!

I'm not kidding, by the time I walked back down the stairs; my daughter retracted everything she had said earlier. She had no idea that I prayed the Word over her and the situation. The Holy Spirit went before me and worked on the problem while I was upstairs confessing His Word aloud. I was sold! Hey, if something works well, you stick with it, right? Now, I'm not saying that it always works instantaneously. My faith is still required. I will say, however, that His peace is instant every time. I continue in peace while confessing His Word over every situation and I don't carry the burden, I leave it with Him. I cast it and He takes care of it. I challenge you to try it out for yourself. Joyce Meyer has a wonderful book called, *The Secret Power of Speaking God's Word*. It is like a promise book, and I recommend it to everyone. I keep several copies on hand in various places. A soldier should never be caught without his sword. March on, Christian soldier and use your offensive weapon to defeat all that isn't of God in your life. Victory in Jesus!

WHO HE IS FOR YOU

Teaching a ladies Bible study for several years has blessed me with awesome fellowship among like-minded women. Over the years we touched on many different areas. The lesson we studied on the names of Jesus has always stayed with me in a comforting way. Do you know who Jesus is for you? As you read His many names you will find that He has left nothing out. When you understand that He is your *everything*, you will be set free from all of the ugliness the world may throw at you. Please, allow me to introduce you to . . .

*Jehovah Yeshua–your Savior

Jesus is our Savior. He came to save us from our sin. "Because if you acknowledge and confess with your lips that Jesus is Lord and in your heart believe (adhere to, trust in and rely on the truth) that God raised Him from the dead, you will be saved" (Romans 10:9 *AMP*). Salvation is free; you need only receive Him into your heart (See 1 John 4:14; John 4:42; Luke 19:10)

*Jehovah Tsidkenu (sid-ken-new)–your Righteousness

Jesus is your Righteousness and because of His shed blood you are in right relationship with the Father. "For he hath made him to be sin for us, who knew no sin; that we might be made the righteousness of God in him" (2 Corinthians 5:21 *KJV*). (See Philippians 3:9; Romans 3:21-24)

*Jehovah M'kaddesh (ma-kad-desh)–your Sanctification

Jesus is your sanctification. He is your sin eraser. He makes you holy through the continuing work of the Holy Spirit in your heart. "And may the God of peace Himself sanctify you through and through (separate you from profane things, make you pure and wholly consecrated to God); and may your spirit and soul and body be preserved sound and complete (and found) blameless at the coming of our Lord Jesus Christ (the Messiah)" (1 Thessalonians 5:23 *AMP*). (See 1 Corinthians 1:30; 2 Thessalonians 2:13; Hebrews 2:11)

*Jehovah Shalom (sha-lome)–your Peace

Jesus is your peace and contentment. He is your freedom from disturbance and fear. "And God's peace (shall be yours, that tranquil state of a soul assured of its salvation through Christ, and so fearing nothing from God and being content with its earthly lot of whatever sort that is, that peace) which transcends all understanding shall garrison and mount guard over your hearts and minds in Christ Jesus" (Philippians 4:7 *AMP*). (See Ephesians 2:13-14; Isaiah 9:6; Psalm 4:8; John 14:27)

*Jehovah Shammah–your ever present Father

Jesus is ever present with us in the form of His Holy Spirit. You see, my friend, as long as you are His, you can *never* be alone. "And I will be a Father to you, and you shall be My sons and daughters, says the Lord Almighty" (2 Corinthians 6:18 *AMP*). Also, the apostle Matthew says, "Teaching them to observe everything that I have commanded you, and behold, I am with you all the days (perpetually, uniformly, and on every occasion), to the (very) close and consummation of the age. Amen (so let it be)" (Matthew 28:20 *AMP*). (See Genesis 28:15; Psalm 46:1; Isaiah 41:10)

*Jehovah Ishi (ye-she)–your Helper

Through the years I have often found myself yelling out for Jesus to help me. Whether for a small incident or a major adversity, our Helper is only a prayer away. "When the righteous cry for help, the Lord hears, and delivers them out of all their distress and troubles" (Psalm 34:17 *AMP*). God is so good to us (See Psalm 28:7; Psalm 50:15; Isaiah 41:13; Isaiah 50:7)

*Jehovah Rapha (rah-fah)–your Healer

Often I pray for sick brothers and sisters. A prayer chain is a powerful thing. Jesus bore our sickness the day He was crucified, and He still heals today. Jesus not only heals our minds and physical ailments, but He heals our relationships as well. "But He was wounded for our transgressions, He was bruised for our guilt and iniquities; the chastisement (needful to obtain) peace and well-being for us was upon Him, and with the stripes (that wounded) Him we are healed and made whole" (Isaiah 53:5 *AMP*). Thanks be to God! (See Matthew 9:35; Luke 6:19; Jeremiah 17:14; Psalm 107:20; Proverbs 4:20-22)

*Jehovah Tosru (sow-ree)–your Strength

"I just can't do this anymore; I am spent, done; it's over!" We have all said that at one time or another. Jesus not only saves us from death and hell but He also saves us from our everyday weakness. When I tap into the Lord's supernatural strength, He is always faithful to pick me up off the ground. "But He said to me, My grace (My favor and loving- kindness and mercy) is enough for you (sufficient against any danger and enables you to bare the trouble manfully); for My strength and power are made perfect (fulfilled and complete) and show themselves most effective in (your) weakness. Therefore, I will all the more gladly glory in my weaknesses and infirmities, that the strength and power of Christ (the Messiah) may rest (yes, may pitch a tent over and dwell) upon me" (2 Corinthians 12:9 *AMP*). We thank you Lord, for holding us up amidst the storms of life. (See Isaiah 40:29; Luke 10:19; Acts 1:8; 1 Corinthians 15:57; Ephesians 3:16; 2 Timothy 1:7)

*Jehovah El Shaddai (shad-eye)–your God that is *more* than enough (All Mighty)

He is the great *I Am*, the all-sufficient One! Jesus is more than enough because He meets our every need and also leaves some left over to share with others. For a season in my life when I thought I was really going to lose it, Christ even became my sanity. Three weeks before the birth of my second child, my mom died suddenly at the age of fifty-one. Then my daughter had to be hospitalized at four days old. Death was so near I could taste it. I literally thought I would be burying my baby as well. He will be for you, what you need Him to be at the moment you need Him! *More* than enough! "And God is able to make all grace (every favor and earthly blessing) come to you in abundance, so that you may always and under all circumstances and whatever the need be self-sufficient (possessing enough to require no aid or support and furnished in abundance for every good work and charitable donation)" (2 Corinthians 9:8 *AMP*). (See Romans 8:32, 37; John 14:13; Ephesians 1:3, 19; Psalm 84:11; Philippians 4:19)

*Jehovah Rohi (row-he)–your Shepherd

To truly understand Jesus as our Shepherd, we need to understand the relationship between the shepherd and his sheep. Years ago I read a book called; *A Shepherd Looks at Psalm 23*, by W. Phillip Keller. I will never again think of Christ my shepherd as simply watching over me. "The Lord is my Shepherd (to feed, guide and shield me), I shall not lack. He makes me lie down in (fresh, tender) green pastures; He leads me beside the still and restful waters. (Revelation 7:17.) He refreshes and restores my life (my self); He leads me in the paths of righteousness (uprightness and right standing with Him–not for my earning it, but) for His name's sake. Yes, though I walk through the (deep, sunless) valley of the shadow of death, I will fear or dread no evil, for You are with me; Your rod (to protect) and Your staff(to guide), they comfort me. You prepare a table before me in the presence of my enemies. You anoint my head with oil; my (brimming) cup runs over. Surely or only goodness, mercy, and unfailing love shall follow me all the days of my life, and through the length of my days the house of the Lord (and His presence) shall be my dwelling place" (Psalm 23:1-6 AMP). What wonderful promises! (See Psalm 91:1-2; Psalm 9:9; Proverbs 14:26; Hebrews 6:18)

*Jehovah Jireh–your Provider

We are truly blessed to live in the U.S.A. I believe with all of my heart that we as a nation want for nothing, because we are such givers. The American people lead the world in charitable contributions. "Give, and (gifts) will be given to you; good measure, pressed down, shaken together, and running over. For with the measure you deal out (with the measure you use when you confer benefits on others), it will be measured back to you" (Luke 6:38 *AMP*). (See Malachi 3:10; Psalm 34:10; Matthew 6:3-4; Deuteronomy 8:18; Deuteronomy 28:8, 11)

*Jehovah Nissi (nee-see)–your Banner

A banner is like a flag. It symbolizes protection, victory and to whom you belong. Jesus our banner unifies us as children of God and soldiers in this fight of faith (1 Timothy 6:12; 2 Timothy 4:7). Jesus our high Commander is the banner that directs our steps and encourages us. Jesus is to Whom we belong. "The Lord is my Rock, my Fortress, and my Deliverer; my God, my keen and firm Strength in Whom I will trust and take refuge, my Shield, and the Horn of my salvation, my High tower. I will call upon the Lord, Who is to be praised; so shall I be saved from my enemies" (Psalm 18:2-3 *AMP*). (See Psalm 32:7; Psalm 18:29; 1 Chronicles 29:11; Psalm 149:4)

There are certainly more names of Jehovah than the ones we studied. However, this study reaffirmed how big our God really is. Often we limit Him, giving Him earthly boundaries. Let us always remember Jesus our intimate Friend. And may we never forget God our Sovereign, Almighty Creator, Who gives us breath and takes it away (Matthew 10:28; Psalm 147:11).

STAY BOYFRIEND
AND GIRLFRIEND

Earlier I discussed the importance of knowing your spiritual gifts. Learning your personality trait is another important step in achieving a healthy, balanced life. My family and I were so enlightened the day we discovered our traits. It brought understanding and a healing acceptance to our family unit. Each trait has a positive side; as well as a negative. The positive is what shines forth in our personalities, but negative traits have to be acknowledged and controlled. There are many detailed resources on this subject. However, I will only touch on them briefly. If you are engaged or a newlywed, I recommend learning one another's traits. It is such a powerful tool toward understanding how the other is wired, and it will avoid many petty arguments.

Personality traits can be broken down into four groups:

- Typically cheerful, talkative and self-centered

- Strong-willed, confident and quick to get angry

- Perfectionist, sensitive and moody

- Calm, dependable and stubborn

There is much more to each of these but you get the idea. The key is to utilize the positive aspects of your personality and work on the negatives.

When your children come along you can observe which type they are and work with them as they mature, by encouraging their strengths. Because I was quick tempered and strong-willed, I was a pain in the neck to live with. You can ask my husband; he'd be happy to tell you all about it. I knew he'd always love me but there was a season in our marriage when we didn't always like each other. But, praise God! He had promised "for worse" and he loved me enough to stick with me until I changed. We all need to be more patient with one another. The same can be said for seasons with our children. You love them always but sometimes you may not like their behavior. Do not fuel the negative side of your spouse or child. If you are aware of what makes them irritated, don't assist by feeding their weaknesses. Instead, help them by nurturing their strengths (Ephesians 6:4).

Early in marriage, we need to have realistic expectations. The same goes for new parents. Knowing yours and your spouse's personality types early on helps to bring stability and understanding to a new and sometimes frustrating experience. When you first started dating you observed each other's positive traits, for the most part. We usually demonstrate our best behavior during this time. Hopefully, if you're engaged long enough, time will expose the negative as well and you will know what to expect. During this time each of you are usually agreeable. He is the faithful knight atop his trusted steed, and you are his beautiful bride whom he adores. Do not allow that to die out completely. Yes, I remember I said to have *realistic* expectations, but in order to keep that spark alive you need to stay *boyfriend* and *girlfriend* throughout your marriage. Continue to give him respect and attention, and he will continue to show you love and affection. If you are going through a season of not liking yourself or your spouse, simply ask Jesus to fill you with His love, until yours catches up. Literally, Christ will give you love for him until yours becomes reignited. I've tested it and it works! During the season of not liking my husband, I realized I didn't really like myself. It affected my behavior negatively and affected everyone around me as well.

The Word of God is like a mirror and in that season I used it to see everyone else's faults but my own (2 Corinthians 3:18). I struggled early in my marriage because of *mommy-itis*, my upbringing and not having a father. I now know better and no longer use the past as an excuse for my bad behavior. It is what it is and I can't move forward while dragging it behind me. Sometimes I think Christians get lazy because we assume our spouses will never leave us anyway. If that's you, shame on you! The marriage relationship takes work. Your relationship with your coworkers, friends and children takes work and your relationship with Christ takes work. Any decent relationship requires your time and attention. God so loved the world that He gave. You love your spouse, so you give of yourself, with balance, honor and respect.

Although it took some time, I like myself now. I like who I have become *in Christ*. My husband likes me too, and it feels wonderful. Being a spouse or parent is a difficult job. It is the hardest job I've ever loved. We all have probably experienced one-sided relationships at one time or another and it feels horrible. There's not a lonelier feeling than being married to someone who rejects you. It's like two roommates simply coexisting, instead of lovers who cherish one another. Do your best with *your part* in your relationships and God will take care of the rest.

EVOLUTION, HEALTH AND RELATIONSHIPS

I presume we have all learned about evolution in school. Darwinian evolution fueled Hitler's racist ideas, and it continues to fuel our thoughts and attitudes. Many folks who believe in evolution do not believe in an intelligent Creator. Do you believe that all life can be explained with a little pond scum and a microscope? If we did, in fact, come from pond scum and not a Creator, then there is no moral compass as a foundation. A poor foundation *always* results in a cracked and dilapidated structure that will crumble and fall over time. With God, there is Divine Authority and an actual beginning. Without a moral compass, there is no absolute truth. Stalin applied this idea, resulting in millions of deaths under Marxism.

Has anyone noticed that the *missing link* is still missing? Personally, I think it takes more faith to believe in evolution than in creation. Besides, who was there billions of years ago? If you're a follower of Christ and you believe that the earth is billions of years old, then you believe that *death and suffering* came before death and suffering.

The Bible tells us that death came *after* Adam and Eve sinned. The time between Adam and Abraham is approximately 2,000, years and most scholars agree that Abraham lived about 4,000 years ago. This makes our earth approximately 6,000 years old, from the days of creation in Genesis to this present time. Since evolution says that death (dinosaurs, cavemen) came billions of years ago, then that contradicts God's infallible Word. Therefore, evolution is a lie and should be discarded. Why is it that we try to fit man's *theories* into God's Word? Is the Bible true simply because we believe it is? No, the Bible is true whether we believe it or not. If man's speculations and hypotheses do not line up with the Word of God, then the hypothesis is wrong and not the other way around. It isn't hard for me to believe that there is someone smarter than we are out there. Just look at the messes we've made throughout history. That is why God sent a Savior. We needed saving . . . big time! I sure wish that common sense was a bit more common, don't you?

Jesus took Genesis as literal history, so we can too. "All scripture is given by inspiration of God, and is profitable for doctrine, for reproof, for correction, for instruction in righteousness" (2 Timothy 3:16 *KJV*). The Bible says that no prophecy ever originated because some man willed it to do so. It never came by human impulse, but men spoke from God who were borne along, (moved and impelled) by the Holy Spirit (2 Peter 1:21 *AMP*). Jesus quoted Genesis in Mark 10:6-7 and again in Matthew 19:4-5. Because Jesus Himself quoted Genesis as fact, so can we.

I stand on the authority of God's Word from Genesis through Revelation. Man's wisdom has permeated the church and has drawn us away from the literal truth and certainty of scripture. God never wanted organized religion; He wants a personal relationship with His creation. He had a relationship with Adam in Genesis and He created a wife for Adam to experience the marriage relationship. Today, like Adam, I also have a relationship with my Creator. So why do I think that belief in evolution destroys relationships? Because it omits the Creator of all relationships. To truly experience balanced health of mind, body and spirit, we must include the original relationship God made with the first human Adam and the relationship between our Creator and us. "Before I formed you in the womb I knew (and) approved of you (as My chosen instrument), and before you were born I separated and set you apart, consecrating you" (Jeremiah 1:5 *AMP*) . . . In order to receive healing in our relationships, it is only common sense to heal the original one, and the rest, will follow.

We are spiritual beings. "Then the Lord formed man from the dust (the same essential chemical elements are found in man and animal life that are in the soil. This scientific fact was not known to man until recent times, but God was displaying it here) of the ground and breathed into his nostrils the breath or spirit of life and man became a living being" (Genesis 2:7 *AMP*). The breath is our spirit man, the real us. We have a mind and we live in a temporary shell called the body of flesh. All three areas deserve our attention in order for our healing to be complete.

God created one race, the human race and we are all relatives of the first humans Adam and Eve. If we, as the human race, use no moral compass in our lives, we should not be surprised how poorly we relate and regard one another. Our children are learning evolution in all of the government-run schools. They are being taught that truth is relative and there is no right and wrong. So what's the result? A free for all! They don't respect authority (God, parents or the law) and they do not respect themselves. Teenage sex and pregnancy is on the rise. In their anguish children are cutting themselves, looking for answers, but their parents have none to give. Mom, Dad empower yourselves! We must have an answer as to why we believe, what we believe (1 Peter 3:15). It is no wonder, why children are confused, because we are. The answers have always been available to us. It is time that we do our part. We have a choice; let's start with our original relationship with Creator God. It is *never* too late; help is only a choice away; and the very next moment is here for us to start anew!

For many years I have been enlightened by an awesome ministry called Answers in Genesis (answersingenesis.org). Our God is the God of science. This ministry teaches about our Creator in great detail, yet with simplicity for a novice like me. I highly recommend it to everyone.

Because of Evolution . . .

Because of Evolution, there is no Creator. Without the Creator, there is no Word of God. Without the Word of God, there is no moral compass. Without a moral compass, there is no right and wrong. Without right and wrong, everything becomes gray. When everything is gray, there is no absolute truth. Without absolute truth, people question love and purpose. Without love, we stop caring and have no personal value. Without value, we destroy ourselves trying to fill the God-shaped hole in our hearts with other things—things like premarital sex, adultery, pornography, drugs, cutting and out-of-wedlock pregnancies. We thirst for attention. We want to be wanted. We want to be loved, even if it isn't genuine. We want unconditional love. Can a baby bring unconditional love? A baby without a married mom and dad offers a false sense of the love that is sought. Daddy is absent while baby grows up. Baby resents Mommy and hates her for his emptiness, dysfunction and lack of identity. So, Baby's unconditional love is temporary—just like the temporary "love" of the baby's father. Both Mother and child are unloved. Now both are alone . . . and the cycle continues.

This way of thinking has never answered life's many questions and has only helped to destroy the very thing we were created to have . . . God's unconditional love and a relationship with the One, who will never reject us, leave us or abandon us (Hebrews 13:5-6).

WHITE FLAG IT

Teaching women and being a woman myself has taught me much about my gender. I believe if you polled 100 women/wives, the majority will say the same thing about men/husbands (and vice versa). Sure we all look different and may have different personalities, but we are all still created *woman*. I think if folks just realized this simple truth, there would be less adultery and divorce. The grass is not always greener on the other side; you still have to fertilize it and pull the weeds. This is what I like to call a *white flag* state of affairs. Why do men and women marry three and four times? Men were created men and women were created women. So, *white flag it*! Surrender to it and love the one you've got.

"Honey, where is the hot sauce I like?"

"It's in the refrigerator, Dear."

"I can't find it Babe!"

"It's in there, Shnookums I just saw it earlier."

"Nope, it's not in there."

"It is in there, just move something; it may be behind something else."

You see, if it's not right in front of most men, they just can't see it. *White flag it*! Wives expect husbands to read their minds. "If he loves me, he should know how I feel. He should be able to sense why I am pouting and ignoring him." *White flag it*. Ladies, men *can't* read minds, so just tell them how you're feeling. Choose your love and love your choice.

My husband and I are at a truly delightful place in our marriage. We are over petty fights and pointless arguments that disrupt the peace in our relationship. We laugh at ourselves often, and we've accepted the way the good Lord made us. Not that we aren't striving to improve ourselves; we're just content with the *us* we've become. We've *white flagged it*, and it is very healing. Through the course of our marriage two words often came up— *never* and *always*. "You *never* spend enough time with me." "You're *always* on the computer." "You're *always* nagging me." "You *never* stop talking." Thank goodness, after all of these years, that type of conversation is few and far between. At this stage in our marriage if either of us uses the infamous *always* and *never* in a sentence, the other quickly points it out, and we have a good laugh about it.

God's grace, time and maturity have simply turned words of war into nonsensical words of laughter. The one who slips up and uses those silly words feels the fool. Because we're so over it, we're at ease in this season of marriage. So many couples don't wait long enough to get to that pleasant place ending up with broken relationships. They usually remarry after a while and realize they have the same problems they had the last time. They should have *white flagged it*. My hubby and I did say "for better or for worse." *Worse* can mean any degree of hardship, from trivial arguments to cancer. Besides, I don't recall observing our best man dragging him kicking and screaming down the aisle. He was sweating a bit though, but, hey we were married in August and in Florida!

I've always hated the saying, *my better half*. I'm half and he's half and together we're whole? What a horrible lie from the pit of hell. So then, if I never married, I would be walking around only half a person? No way! I am 100% me, whole, healthy and complete. I have value and purpose all on my own because my Creator made me that way. Can I get an amen? Isn't that the problem with young people today? They feel that they are no one without someone. They have to have a boyfriend or girlfriend to feel special or worthwhile. Hey, you *are* someone special; no other person is required. The Lord created you wonderfully, inside your mother's womb. We need to instill this into our children so that they will not look to any old Tom, Dick or Harry (Jane, Sue or Margie) to fill their value and purpose void. Teaching our children who they are in Christ is vitally important to a healthy mindset and spiritual peace.

I need to insert here that perfection is a *white flagger*. Personally I tried to fit into those shoes and nearly imploded under the pressure. With Christ's strength and the Holy Spirits' guidance we are to strive for holiness everyday (1 Peter 1:15). But we can only do this through the surrendered life, with humility and submission to the only One who is perfect, Jesus, Emmanuel. He is the only perfect thing about us (1 Corinthians 3:16-19).

At the writing of this book I have been married twenty-four years. I want to encourage you to hold on to your marriage. My eyes are droopy, my wrinkles are deeper and my hair gets grayer every year, likewise that of my husband. Yet, when I look into his eyes, I still see him as the man I made a promise to back in 1987. I don't have to look twenty-one again. I have my man and he has his woman, and together we'll grow old gracefully. The key to our long and happy marriage is communication, negotiation, and learning to laugh at ourselves. We will try to enjoy each season of life with each other, for better or for worse, in sickness and in health, till death. Obviously, we didn't start out this content with ourselves and each other. But, we were patient long enough and loved each other enough to get through all the tough times. Those trials made us who we are.

So I encourage you—don't give up right before the victory is sealed. If you are praying for your marriage or child to change, then wield your sword as you come boldly to the throne, for power from on high. God is the only one who can change the heart of a person; our job is to speak the Word over them. You take care of the vertical (your relationship with God) and He will take care of the horizontal (your relationship with others). The only way to achieve healthy balanced relationships is to learn when to *white flag* things that we don't have the power to change.

Do it for the Children

The most important thing you can do for your child's health is to start early. By Training their palates to enjoy *real* food while they're young, you are going to make your job a lot easier. Your toddler's brain will be fed the required nutrition, which will make for a calmer child. Your teen will be fueled with the proper nutrition to keep hormones in balance and keep mood swings in check. We cannot expect our bodies to respond to life properly when the cells have not been fed what they require. Actually, you can go back even further by making sure that Mom and Dad are consuming God-made foods and keeping fit long before conception. Healthy parents make healthy offspring.

Our children eat whatever we buy for them. A five-year-old cannot drive by himself to a fast-food restaurant. We are successfully training up our children in the ways of the world (Proverbs 22:6). Yet our children need to be taught to honor God in their bodies, which belong to Him. We often warn them about smoking, drinking, drugs and premarital sex. But I took it a step further to include man-made chemicals, additives, preservatives and the like. God never intended for us to put that stuff into our bodies. My family and I have reaped peace of mind, body and spirit simply by returning to foods that God created for us to consume. We trained our children early and have saved thousands of dollars on doctor bills and prescriptions. Praise the Lord! We are living proof that this stuff works.

When my friend's son started second grade he contracted strep throat. After a throat culture, the doctor prescribed the usual round of antibiotics. She completed the treatment just as the doctor ordered, only to have a repeat diagnosis the following month. This happened several times. Finally, my friend had enough. When her son came down with strep throat again, she was determined not to suppress the fever and let it run its course naturally.

The fever lasted approximately four days and yes, he missed some school, but he never got strep again! Testimonies like this one are too numerous to count. Parents are pummeling children with antibiotics and over-the-counter drugs. Whatever happened to applying a little menthol rub on their chest and running the vaporizer? Whatever happened to a hot cup of chamomile tea and a teaspoon of honey? My mom couldn't afford to take us to the doctor because we didn't have much; we had no choice but to let our self-healing bodies do their thing.

On a completely different note, I'd like to add that a child who feels valued is a healthier child. Verbal toxins, such as, "You're stupid, worthless and will never amount to anything," are very destructive. This type of behavior quickly closes your child's spirit and the wall around him gradually becomes impenetrable. The old saying that *a child should be seen and not heard* is equally destructive. In order for the child to respect the parent, the parent needs to be respectable. "Do as I say and not as I do," is yet another caustic approach. You will only make yourself untrustworthy and a liar in their eyes. Our daughters trust my husband and me because we are people of our word. There is a powerful sense of security for them in knowing this. What our growing children thought, said and felt mattered to us. It mattered not only because they were on loan to us by their Creator, but because we know that the same Holy Spirit indwells them as it does us. We are all children of God, created in His image and likeness (Genesis 1:26). Now don't get me wrong, I do not advocate becoming your child's friend until they're out of the house. They have plenty of friends and only two parents. We treat our children like they have worth. We respect them as fellow believers and human beings on this earth.

With our consistency in parenting and actually doing what we say, whether it's following through with a punishment or going to an event, we won't say it unless we mean it. When you sow this type of upbringing into your family, you reap secure, peaceful and balanced children. Our girls are not perfect by any stretch of the imagination and neither are we. But raising them has been much more sweet than bitter, because we intentionally raised them with stability of mind (truth, value, purpose), body (nutrition to feed mind and body), and spirit (pointing them to the Prince of peace in hopes that they will choose Him too).

As parents we make our jobs much harder than it needs to be. Do not accept word curses like the *terrible twos* and *teenage rebellion*. Those are lies from the father of lies (John 8:44). Fill your home, mind, body and spirit with the good things of God and you too will reap the balance and peace of all He has promised in His Holy Word.

SAYING GRACE

Thank you Father for this food . . . Bless us, oh Lord, and these Thy gifts . . .
God is great, God is good . . .

". . . Foods which God created to be received with thanksgiving by those who believe and have (an increasingly clear) knowledge of the truth. For everything God has created is good, and nothing is to be thrown away or refused if it is received with thanksgiving. For it is hallowed and consecrated by the Word of God and by prayer" (1 Timothy 4:3-5 *AMP*).

Did God make soda, chips and candy? The Bible says for everything *God has created* is good, not what man has created or tainted in some way. It is sanctified, not by prayer (the blessing, grace) alone. "Lord, bless this fried doughnut. May it nourish my body. Amen!" It is sanctified by the Word of God first, then prayer. What does the Word of God say? It says that what *He* has created is good and to be received with thanksgiving.

I have a tough time praying for God to bless unhealthy, harmful foods. If you eat fried food every day for breakfast, lunch and dinner for three months and pray a blessing over it before you consume it, you will still gain weight and clog your arteries. God is not mocked; you will reap what you sow (Galatians 6:7-8). Do we truly expect God to miraculously change the unhealthy foods into something that will nourish our bodies? Our relationship with Him is based on our freedom to choose; He did not create us robots. We have our part to do in this two-part relationship.

"What agreement (can there be between) a temple of God and idols? For we are the temple of the living God; even as God said, I will dwell in and with and among them and will walk in and with and among them, and I will be their God, and they shall be My people. So, come out from among (unbelievers), and separate (sever) yourselves from them, says the Lord, and touch not (any) unclean thing; then I will receive you kindly and treat you with favor. And I will be a Father to you, and you shall be My sons and daughters, says the Lord Almighty. Therefore, since these (great) promises are ours, beloved, let us cleanse ourselves from everything that contaminates and defiles body and spirit, and bring (our) consecration to completeness in the (reverential) fear of God" (2 Corinthians 6:16–7:1 *AMP*).

The Word tells us to cleanse ourselves from *everything* that contaminates and defiles the body. We often take that to mean only alcohol, drugs, and tobacco. But our American diets are loaded with contaminants. Obesity is everywhere and even some four-year-olds have plaque in their arteries! We bring it upon ourselves by our worldly food choices. We are not coming out from among them. We are not separating ourselves from the way the world eats. We were created to eat and live a certain way–God's way!

God receives glory when we take care of our bodies by fueling it correctly. Now that doesn't mean that you can *never* go out to eat or go to your Grandmother's for Thanksgiving dinner. I'm talking about our everyday food. Make *treat* time just that, a treat. A treat is an unusual gratification and not an everyday occurrence. The body can handle the occasional cookie. But beat up the body during breakfast, lunch and dinner for years, and it will give in and eventually give up. It's really just common sense. It never ceases to amaze me how much our bodies can take until it can't take anymore. Some time ago I saw a TV show about a 1,000 pound man! Wow, that guy's body took everything he gave it–until one day his body couldn't take anymore. That is like slow suicide with a fork. So sad and so preventable. *My friend, if you ignore your health, it will go away.*

MERRY MEDICINE

*"A happy heart is good medicine and a cheerful mind works
healing, but a broken spirit dries up the bones"*

Proverbs 17:22

So, here goes . . .

~Which vegetable needs diapers? *Leeks*

~What kind of vegetable is always in trouble? *Kelp!*

~Which grain has a foul mouth? *Bulgur wheat*

Okay, so you either laughed, cracked a smile or rolled your eyes . . . Ha!

Did you know that when we laugh, natural chemicals called endorphins are released by our brain? They improve mood, relieve pain and it give us an all around good feeling. Laughter is just one of many things we can incorporate into our lives, to restore balance. We were created to laugh! I think the Lord has a sense of humor, and as I age I'm more convinced. I have learned to laugh at myself when I mess up instead of getting angry. The enemy would love to rob me of my joy because he knows the joy of the Lord is my strength. So if we allow him to steal our strength, then we'll be weak enough to believe his lies (Nehemiah 8:10).

"All the days of the desponding and afflicted are made evil (by anxious thoughts and forebodings), but he who has a glad heart has a continual feast (regardless of the circumstances)" (Proverbs 15:15 *AMP*). If you're waiting for your life to be perfect before you can be happy, you'll be waiting forever. There is no such thing as a perfect life as long as you live in a sinful, imperfect world. But, in Christ we can be glad of heart because we who believe in Him have our names written in the Lamb's book of life. We have a permanent home in glory, with a perfect Father Who awaits us. Now that is something to be happy about!

Another important way that I've learned to obtain happiness is by putting others before me. I got better through benevolence. My husband and I lived in Saudi Arabia for several years. We were blessed to travel on that side of the globe and experience life in other countries. We are so thankful for all our travel experiences. They have made a huge impact on how we view the *big picture*. Many Americans don't realize how blessed we are as a nation. I've often felt that if anyone had a problem with the U.S., they should take a trip to one of the poorer nations. They would never be the same again. Some of our poorest people would be their richest. So if you have the opportunity to go on a mission's trip or to visit a third-world country, I highly recommend it. It will change you for the better, and you will never regret it.

The self-centered attitude is noxious. Selfishness puts a person in the #1 position at all times. "She who lives in pleasure and self-gratification (giving herself up to luxury and self indulgence) is dead even while she (still) lives," (1 Timothy 5:6 *AMP*). Webster's dictionary says that a selfish person is devoted unnecessarily to self for private advantage. That is a lonely place to be, and no good can ever come from it. "He who gives to the poor will not want, but he who hides his eyes (from their want) will have many a curse" (Proverbs 28:27 *AMP*). A curse? Wow, that is something we should not take lightly. Giving to the poor doesn't always have to mean monetarily, we can give of our time or talents as well.

Over the years I have found that it really is more blessed to give, than receive (Acts 20:35). When you truly experience the power of giving, you cannot put a price tag on the *high* you'll experience. We are called to look outside ourselves. We are told to, "Bear (endure, carry) one another's burdens and troublesome moral faults, and in this way fulfill and observe perfectly the law of Christ (the Messiah) and complete what is lacking (in your obedience to it). For if any person thinks himself to be somebody (too important to condescend to shoulder another's load) when he is nobody (of superiority except in his own estimation), he deceives and deludes and cheats himself" (Galatians 6:2-3 *AMP*). When we strive to be Christ-centered and not self-centered, only then are we genuinely happy. JOY is found in this order– *Jesus*Others*You.

NATURAL BEAUTY

As I age, I find myself looking for ways to reverse it. In my twenties I used to do my hair and makeup, look into the mirror and say, "That's enough, I look good." Nowadays, I do my hair and makeup and gaze down into my case and try to figure out what else I can do to improve the situation. However, I don't look on the outside like I feel on the inside. I think aging is a humbling experience; yet I wouldn't change all that I've learned for my naive youth. The truth of the matter is that if you're not old, you're dead! I can't go back and become twenty-three again, but I can be my best now.

In my experience, I have found that physical beauty can be obtained internally. On a spiritual note, a Godly woman is beautiful no matter her age. "Charm and grace are deceptive, and beauty is vain (because it is not lasting), but a woman who reverently and worshipfully fears the Lord, she shall be praised" (Proverbs 31:30 AMP). Have you ever met an attractive man or woman, who had a sour disposition and instantly their appearance became ugly? The internal beauty of a man and woman of God becomes even more beautiful with age. A healthy inside creates a healthy outside, spiritually as well as physically. For example, eating God's way helps our skin stay clear and soft. Meditating on the promises of God removes stress. Exercise aids our appearance by looking fit and shapely.

Often infomercials for cosmetics claim to enhance beauty, reduce the appearance of wrinkles or even reverse aging. I say, "Don't waste your hard earned money." Even the most beautiful movie stars of the 40's and 50's are wrinkled and old today, and they probably had the means to buy the best products. Certainly if you're buying makeup, lotion, toners and creams, you should look for natural ingredients. The skin is our largest organ and whatever you put on it gets absorbed into your body. So, let me get back to the infomercials. They often tout products that have miracle melons, oils or fruits that are supposed to erase signs of aging. Why not slap some melon directly onto your skin? Why buy a $100 one-ounce cream that probably has .001% melon in it, when you can rub fresh melon right onto your face! No kidding, many of the fruits God created contain ingredients that help us to look our best. If healthy foods can do wonderful things for us internally, then why not externally?

The acid found in lemons remove dulling residue that may build up on hair. Coconut oil is a natural moisturizer for hair and skin. It also helps aid digestion, along with many other benefits too numerous to mention. Pomegranate is high in vitamin C and is said to protect against skin conditions. Kiwi fruit has natural renewing properties that soothe skin. The enzymes in papaya rid skin of old cells and assist in creating new ones. Olive oil is a wonderful moisturizer for rough hands, elbows and knees. Oatmeal soothes irritated skin. Baking soda can be used as a mild abrasive to lift off dead skin and whiten teeth. You get the idea. We've all seen those ladies with the cucumbers on their eyes. If many of these foods are found in the ingredient list of expensive lotions, then there has to be something to it. So, apply the healthy foods directly onto your skin and reap the benefits naturally and inexpensively. I do it myself. I'm not kidding! Just do me a favor and check the mirror before you leave the house . . .

HEALTHFUL HINTS

1. Avoid cooking with aluminum pots, pans and foil; they may leak aluminum into the food. Aluminum has been linked to Alzheimer's disease. I use glass, ceramic, wrought iron and stainless steel.

2. Do not use aerosol cans. Some of them contain chemical propellants which may cause cancer. Use the pump type spray bottles instead.

3. Many household cleaners are toxic. I use a white vinegar and water solution for mirrors, glass and counter tops. I use straight white vinegar (the cheap stuff) when I need to kill bacteria on surfaces. I use baking soda to scrub sinks, toilets and tubs. Used together their foaming action cleans away most stubborn stains.

4. Buy dye and fragrance-free products. Soap, shampoo, lotion and toilet paper touch the body and should not contain harmful additives.

5. Bring the outdoors in. Indoor plants help to clean household air and they give off life-giving oxygen. Be careful to keep poisonous plants up high away from children and pets. Be sure to dust the leaves periodically.

6. Check your toothpaste for saccharin. It's the same stuff in those sugar packets. Not too long ago they had a cancer warning on saccharin packets. Never consume artificial man-made sugar of any kind.

7. Sit away from your TV and computer screens they have EMF's (electromagnetic field). Anything that you plug in has an EMF. The

farther you are from them the better. Do not allow your children to sit close to the TV/computer and be sure to teach them why.

8. Check your home for Radon. And make the necessary changes to correct it if your home has unhealthy levels. Radon is a radioactive gas from the decay of uranium in the soil.

9. Do not use old ceramic pottery to serve food, it may contain lead.

10. Have your tap water checked for contaminants. I distill my own drinking water at home. I have also replaced my shower head with one that has a carbon filter, so that I will not absorb chlorine and other contaminants.

11. Chocolate has caffeine. Try carob instead.

12. Coffee and tea contain caffeine. Try herbal tea, but be sure and read the labels as some of them contain artificial ingredients.

13. Stay away from refined white sugar; instead substitute it for, dates, raisins, honey, agave, Sucanat (brand name; unrefined cane sugar) or pure maple syrup.

14. Most canned veggies and fruits have no nutritional value, use fresh instead. Frozen fruits and veggies come in second. Wipe off can top before opening; they're filthy!

15. Imported cans may contain lead solder. Most don't, but a simple way to check is to run your finger along the solder line. If it is crooked or bumpy it may be lead. When in doubt, throw it out!

16. I have learned that garlic is a natural antibiotic. It is also said to reduce cholesterol and blood pressure and it has anti-cancer properties. So eat it in good health.

17. Squeeze fresh lemon into your purified drinking water. It is supposed to be a natural liver cleanser, not to mention increasing your vitamin C intake.

18. Do you get motion sickness when traveling? Try powdered ginger capsules, it really works for me. I get to read in the car when I take my ginger.

19. Raw unfiltered honey is a natural antiseptic. My friend, who is a chiropractor, used it on a wound that his mom had. For some reason, other remedies didn't help until he applied raw honey directly on the wound for several days. God's medicine!

20. Unsulphured blackstrap molasses is naturally high in iron and calcium. My girls and I would often take a few tablespoons after our menstrual cycle if we felt a little sluggish. It does the trick.

21. Exercise strengthens your immunity. More than once when I have felt a cold coming on, I would take vitamin C and a garlic capsule, then I'd jump on my elliptical for 5-10 minutes and the symptoms would disappear. No kidding!

22. Our bodies are approximately 70% water. By the time you *feel* thirsty, you're probably already dehydrated. We need to try our best and drink half of our body weight in ounces of water daily. For example if I am 100 pounds, than I should drink 50 ounces of water a day or approximately 7, 8 oz. glasses. This number needs to increase when you exercise.

23. Don't expect your children to eat less junk food if you don't! They learn by example.

24. Avoid the 4 whites! White flour, sugar, salt (sodium chloride) and fat.

25. Consume God-made brown rice not man-altered white rice.

26. When dining out for Chinese food make sure you ask for no MSG (monosodium glutamate) in your dish. Many restaurants automatically use it in their buffets.

27. Try mint or ginger tea for an upset stomach.

28. Try a digestive plant enzyme supplement for gas pains. It works for us.

29. Consume beans and legumes for your fiber and protein intake. Beans are *meat* in our family.

30. Soda may rob your bones of calcium, among other things.

31. Man-made sweeteners have been linked to arthritis. My girlfriend had arthritis in her forties. She consumed a lot of foods with a popular man-made sweetener in it. She didn't change her diet but totally avoided the artificial sweetener, and the arthritis disappeared. She gave this testimony herself, and it is no surprise to me.

32. Breast feeding/pregnant moms may pass toxins onto babies if they ingest foods laden with them. You and Baby truly are what you eat.

33. Foods labeled sugar-free or non-fat are usually loaded with chemicals.

34. I've learned that Americans consume approximately 7 pounds of chemicals per year.

35. Avoid sunburns and tanning beds. They lead to premature aging. I am now seeing the results of my Florida tans from back in my 20's. Boo hoo!

36. Be aware of pollution in your neighborhood. Don't buy a home close to power lines (EMF's) or factories with smoke stacks.

37. Stop biking, jogging or running on traffic-filled streets. You are breathing in large amounts of carbon monoxide!

38. Discuss with your children/grandchildren why many of the foods advertised on TV are unhealthy. Advertisers don't care about your health; they only want your money.

39. Charcoal grilled or BBQ foods may contain carcinogens.

40. Teach your children God's dietary principals.

41. Avoid radiated and genetically modified (GMO) foods. Eat only unaltered God-made foods.

42. Grow your own organic garden. It's easier than you think. When I garden, I always give 10-15% to the bugs.

43. Milk, dairy, eggs and meats may be tainted with veterinary drugs (e.g. hormones and antibiotics).

44. Too much fluoride has been linked to cancer. My girls grew up on well water and my dentist wanted to give them fluoride drops. I refused. I'd rather have cavities than chemo! They both have lovely, strong chops.

45. Microwaves should be banned from a healthy home. They change/alter the food and may emit radiation.

46. Unlined copper pots can release too much copper into foods causing vomiting and diarrhea.

47. Avoid harsh fumes, smoke, perfume, cleaners . . . especially when young lungs are present.

48. Install smoke and/or carbon monoxide detectors in your home.

49. Do not use margarine. It is one molecule shy of becoming plastic!

50. Do not use hydrogenated or partially hydrogenated oils. Read your Labels.

51. Use those green bags or containers when storing produce. They keep produce fresher longer and, in turn, saves you money.

52. Buy stainless steel or glass water bottles (no aluminum or plastic). The plastic can leach into the water, especially when left in a hot car.

53. Do not use canola oil. It is made from the genetically engineered rapeseed plant. Rapeseed is high in erucic acid and makes a wonderful insect repellent.

54. If you wake up in the morning with very puffy eyes, try decreasing your salt intake and increasing your water intake.

55. Never combine bleach and ammonia–a deadly combination! Use natural less toxic cleaners in your home.

56. Pressed wood furniture/cabinets may leach formaldehyde. Emissions of formaldehyde have been linked to cancer. Seal furniture well with polyurethane (ventilate well) or replace with natural wood furniture.

57. Plastic vinyl blinds/shower curtains and children's blow-up toys emit a toxic smell. Replace the vinyl blinds with aluminum. Completely air out the plastic curtain and toys outdoors before using it.

58. Do not freeze plastic water bottles. The plastic leaches into the water. At least one report states it has been found in the breast tissue of women.

59. Granite countertops may emit radon.

60. Always use the air re-circulation button in your car. This will keep the carbon monoxide from other vehicles, out of your car and lungs.

*There are so many things we cannot control. So let's try to do what we can, when we are able. I encourage you to investigate these hints on your own and learn about each one in more detail (Hosea 4:6). To your health!

My Medicine Cabinet

Oscillococcinum (brand name)–I haven't gotten the flu in many years, but I'm never without this homeopathic remedy. During my transition from the standard American diet my body was more prone to sickness. I used this remedy and it really worked to shorten the duration. It is best taken at first onset of symptoms. Now that my oldest daughter is in college (eating who knows what) I keep it on hand, just in case.

Homeopathic remedies (alternative medicine)–When my girls were young and I was a bit "fever phobic" I would keep a children's homeopathic kit on hand. It contained a variety of remedies and instructions.

Garlic capsules–I probably would've had colds more often if not for my garlic capsules. Not to mention (being Italian) how often I cook with it. During the winter months I tended to steer more toward hot, cooked foods making myself more acidic and in turn prone to colds. If I felt a slight cold coming on, a 500 mg capsule typically helped to keep it away.

Vitamin C (preferably from a whole food source)–Vitamin C has the same story as the garlic for me. I would take 1,000 mg if I felt a cold coming on. The juicing of citrus fruit, kiwi and broccoli will also add quality amounts of vitamin C to your diet.

All natural lip balm–I use these often especially in the winter and before bed. Look for all natural ingredients without petroleum based oils, preservatives, flavors and colors. Lip balm goes directly onto your lips and is typically ingested, so make sure it is pure.

Non-petroleum menthol chest rub–This is similar to the stuff Mom used on me when I was all stuffed up, but without the petroleum (from fossil fuels) and other risky ingredients.

Tea Tree oil–This is an oil made from the Melaleuca tree. It can be a bit expensive but a little goes a long way. I have used this to heal ringworm. I used a moistened swab full and dabbed it on the ringworm, and covered it with gauze every day until it was gone. It took approximately 3 weeks to disappear. It is a natural antifungal and can also be used on athlete's feet.

Ginger root powder (capsules)–I don't travel without it! For some reason (after my children were born) I can no longer read in the car without getting motion sickness. Now I take 2 capsules before a long drive and can read from 4-6 hours without nausea. I also use it for plane trips. It has worked wonders for my daughters and me.

Calendula cream, liquid or gel–This cream is made from the marigold flower and can be found in most health food stores. I used it on my daughter's eczema, dry skin and common skin irritations. It soothed the outside while nutrient rich foods healed from within.

Aloe Vera plant–This plant is often referred to as the medicine plant. You can purchase these plants just about anywhere. In colder zones they live best indoors. I also used this on my daughters' eczema, cuts and scrapes.

Liquid vitamin E–My young girls often picked at their scabs. I worried they would create scars by not allowing the wound to heal properly. I'd apply the oil directly on the cut and it aided in the healing process with less scarring. I also use it on my wrinkles and they seem to appear smoother (buy d-alpha tocopherol not *dl*-alpha tocopherol a synthetic form).

PH testing tape–This is a color-coded paper, that helps determine the pH level of your saliva or urine. I use this tape to gauge if I'm eating wisely. As I increase the alkaline forming foods in my diet, I can literally watch as pH levels improve with this tape. It is a visual aid that helps keep my family on the right track.

Raw honey and raw vinegar cough syrup–When I was growing up, my Italian Mom made a honey and scotch fermented syrup for sore throats. I'm not sure if it helped the sore throat or if it just knocked me for a loop so that I wouldn't feel anything. A tablespoon each of raw honey and raw vinegar mixed together and swallowed slowly, helps to soothe a sore throat.

Chamomile tea–My girls have never had much trouble sleeping (after their newborn months). I attribute that to a lot of fresh air, exercise and staying away from sweets, soda and caffeinated beverages. However, when they were under the weather or if their little internal clocks were off, I'd steep them a nice cup of chamomile tea to relax them and aid their sleep.

Aloe Vera rub/gel– Occasionally, my active family would get sore muscles. This gel helped to soothe them, while I massaged the area.

All natural moisturizers/lotions–Read your labels to be sure lotions are made with all natural ingredients without perfumes or dyes. Natural oils soften dry winter skin. Olive, sunflower, almond and safflower oil are all good moisturizers. We like to use mint lotion on our feet to revive them.

Warm olive oil for earaches–Only one of my girls has had an earache and only one time. A few drops of warm olive oil in her sore ear along with a warm hot water bottle, comforted her when it hurt the most. I've also used a drop of hydrogen peroxide in the ear to help loosen ear wax. Just tilt your head to drain and clean out the wax gently with a soft swab. The fizzing sound is normal and will pass.

Natural Calamine lotion (Phenol-free)–I used this often when the girls came down with chicken pox. I also used some homeopathic remedies. My Gram would make an X with her nail onto my mosquito bites to keep them from itching. She would also rub a dampened bar of soap on the bites to alleviate the itch. It really helped.

Activated charcoal tablets–I was lucky enough to get food poisoning 2 times–yuck! After the first bout, I learned about the absorbing power of activated charcoal tablets. The second time was much easier because the charcoal absorbed the toxins from my system. It will turn your stools dark, so don't be alarmed.

Natural citronella bug repellent (natural oil or pump spray)–I use this on my family on those late summer nights to help keep biting insects at bay. Please, do not spray your babies with toxic insect repellents. They are poison! I also recommend a bat house in your yard. Bats eat thousands of mosquitoes a night.

Enema bag–Do you remember those old fashioned red enema bags? I have used warm water to irrigate my colon during times of prolonged constipation. Warm regular coffee is also good to use as an enema, for occasional constipation. The caffeine stimulates the colon to release the compacted feces. It seems we are using coffee for the wrong end. However, if you are on a mostly raw diet, constipation should be a thing of the past.

Hot water bottle–For occasional aches, pains and discomfort from gas, a hot water bottle placed directly on the area does wonders.

Arnica Montana (homeopathic medicine)–A few years ago I had my mercury fillings removed and replaced with porcelain amalgams. My old mercury fillings were leaking toxic poison into my system. I took Arnica before and after both of my 4-hour visits and hardly had any pain during or afterward. So why would I take an over-the-counter drug, when this alterative worked great.

Plant enzyme supplement–I take these when I have eaten too many cooked foods in a day. When I take plant enzymes it helps keep my body from overworking and aids in digestion. A good enzyme blend may include Protease (breaks down protein), Amylase (breaks down starch), Lipase (breaks down fat), Cellulase (breaks down fiber), Lactase (breaks down milk sugar), and Papain and Bromelain, primarily protein digesting enzymes. I personally use a brand by Hallelujah Acres.

Raw juice powders–When I travel or don't take the time to juice raw foods, I supplement with a blend of barley grass, beet and carrot juices in powder form. Be sure to purchase a brand processed to keep the living enzymes intact. It is an easy way to give my body living goodness when time is short. I personally use the Hallelujah Acres brand. I use their Barley Max powder as my "multi vitamin" and I take it 1-3 times a day.

All natural colon cleanser–If I *cheat* on holidays or vacation, I like to give my colon a spring cleaning with a natural colon cleanser. Most cleansers have a psyllium husk base with other fiber and herbs added. I use a Hallelujah Acres brand that has over 25 herbs in it. This colon cleanser sweeps my colon clean and helps it to function properly.

Flax seed–I use ground flax seed every morning. I often buy the whole seed and grind it myself in a coffee grinder (a new use for this appliance). Flax seed is said to lower cholesterol and blood pressure among other things. It really is a wonder food. Flax seed has essential fats that along with exercise have made my monthly mood swings disappear. I take it for myself and my family.

B12–We use a sublingual (dissolve slowly under the tongue) form of B12. We need B vitamins for normal brain function and a healthy nervous system. Supplementing reassures me that we are not in any way deficient.

Organic raw apple cider vinegar–It is best to look for the brand that has *mother* in it. Mother is a cloudy sediment within the vinegar. It has a host of vitamins and minerals. It is good for fighting fungal and bacterial infections. We also use it directly on our skin when needed.

Organic extra virgin coconut oil–This works wonders internally as well as externally. It is a natural antibacterial, antifungal and antioxidant. It also aids in digestion and builds immunity. I take it internally and I also use it on my wrinkles, dry skin and lips.

*My medicine cabinet has changed with each season of life. I no longer need non-petroleum diaper cream. But I'm thankful to the Lord, that my cabinet does not contain any over-the-counter or prescription drugs, simply because we do not need them.

MY SPICE RACK

*Easy to grow in a garden

Agar Agar–a gelatin-like substance derived from red sea weed. It is available in strips or flakes. Used for thickening or jelling foods.

Allspice–actually one spice has a flavor resembling cloves, cinnamon and nutmeg. Use in fruitcake, cookies and many baked goods.

Anise–an aromatic seed that has a licorice-like flavor. Use in cookies, cakes and relish; like chutney (Indian relish).

Basil*–this herb is a must for Italian cooking. It has a sweet, warm, minty flavor and compliments most tomato-based recipes. Use in tomato sauce, pesto, soups, veggies and dressings.

Bay leaf–this herb has a sweet, floral, spicy taste. Use in soups, stews and sauces. My spaghetti sauce and soup would not be nearly as tasty, if I omitted this herb.

Caraway seed–this seed has an anise and dill taste combination. Use in sauerkraut, noodles, dumplings, potatoes and German dishes. I love to add caraway to my homemade bread.

Cardamom seed (green)–a small pod from the ginger family; a strong aromatic flavor used in many Indian dishes. This can be found in Asian markets.

Cayenne pepper*–a hot spice made from dried ground cayenne peppers. Use in salsa, veggie and tomato soups, potato and macaroni salad, coleslaw, stews, dips and spreads.

Celery seed–dried brown seeds of the celery vegetable; the flavor is a bit more intense. Use in salad dressing, salads, soups or anywhere a celery taste is desired. It is a wonderful addition to any dish, when you don't have celery on hand.

Chili powder–made from ground chilies, very hot and spicy. Use in hot salsa, Indian dishes, chili, in place of black pepper, spicy stir fries, soup and anywhere you'd like a kick!

Chives*–an herb belonging to the onion family, resembles thick strands of grass. Use in salads, wraps, baked potatoes and anywhere you'd like a mild onion flavor.

Cilantro*–a leafy herb that resembles parsley when fresh. Use in Mexican, Spanish and Latin American dishes. My raw salsa recipe would not be caught without it.

Cinnamon–ground bark of the cinnamon tree. Use in a variety of baked goods and desserts.

Cloves–a spice from the dried flower of the clove tree can be used whole or ground. Use in various baked goods and my holiday wassail.

Crushed red (pizza) **pepper**–dried hot red pepper flakes with seeds. Use in my lentil stew, sauce, salsa and my pizza salad recipe.

Cumin–aromatic spice with a musky taste. It can be found in powder and seed form. Use in Mexican dishes, soup, chili and my hummus recipe.

Curry powder–a blend of mustard, coriander, turmeric, cumin and red pepper. Used in many Indian recipes.

Dill*–this herb has a fresh pickle aroma. Use in potato salad, pasta salad, soup, sauerkraut, veggies and, of course, pickles.

Dried kelp powder–dried and granulated ocean seaweed. Use in my mock tuna salad, soups and anywhere you'd like a taste of the sea.

Dry mustard–the ground-up seeds of the mustard plant. Use in casseroles and dressing; may be used in place of prepared mustard in some recipes.

Fennel–has the look of short celery, with a bulb bottom. It has a strong licorice flavor. Use in Italian dishes and antipasto salad; tastes lovely raw. It sweetens the breath too.

Ginger–a pungent root often used in Indian and Chinese cooking. Try sucking on a small piece to freshen your breath. Careful . . . there's a kick!

Granulated garlic–dried or dehydrated garlic cloves ground into a powder. Use in everything Italian, salad dressing, veggies, stew, soup, dip. I use it in almost everything. Try it on homemade air popped popcorn for a zing!

Indian blends (garam masala)–a blend of coriander, chili, cumin, clove, fennel, black cardamom, bay leaf, stone flower and anistar. Use in many Indian dishes.

Italian seasoning–a blend of oregano, marjoram, thyme, basil, rosemary and sage. Use in stew, sauces, veggie dishes, soup and my holiday stuffing.

Marjoram–from the mint family. It smells a bit like sage and can be used interchangeably for the most part. Use in soup, stew, stuffing, sauces and herb bread.

Mint*–there are hundreds of varieties of mint. We like to pick right out of the garden and eat them. Minty fresh! Use to flavor dressing, desserts and hot or cold herbal tea.

Naturally harvested sea salt–natural source, unrefined and unbleached. It contains natural trace minerals, usually hand-harvested and naturally evaporated off the Mediterranean coast. Use sparingly whenever salt is desired. I do not use man-made refined table salt (sodium chloride).

Nutmeg–a brown spice that reminds me of the holidays. It is actually a seed and not a nut. It is usually sold whole (more expensive) or in powder form. If you have a recipe that calls for mace, you can easily substitute it for nutmeg; they are very similar in taste. Use in pies, cookies, cakes and some veggie dishes like kale.

Onion powder–finely ground dehydrated onion. Use anywhere you'd use fresh onion.

Oregano*–a mild and slightly bitter herb from the mint family. Use in Italian dishes, my tomato sauce recipe, soup, stew and veggies of all kinds. It is best to grow oregano in a pot; it may "take over" other herbs.

Paprika–a sweet mild red pepper with a lovely red color. Use in Hungarian dishes, salad, veggies, my cabbage and noodles. It also makes a wonderful garnish for a finished dish.

Parsley*–an aromatic herb with crinkly or flat leaves that have a bright, fresh flavor. Use in soup, stew, sauces, dip or garnish. A bit of fresh parsley added at the end of most food preparation will add a wonderful fresh taste!

Rosemary*–a sweet-tasting herb that is similar to sage. Use in stew, stuffing, veggies and soup.

Tarragon–a green herb with thin pointed leaves. The flavor has a hint of anise. Use in pasta dishes and salad dressing.

Thyme*–an herb with small, dark green aromatic leaves. Use in stew, soup, stuffing and veggies.

Turmeric–a root from the ginger family with a vibrant yellow color (Be careful. This spice will stain).Turmeric is what makes mustard bright yellow. Use in Indian and curry dishes, sauces and dressing. I have used this as a natural food coloring.

100% real vanilla–an extract of the vanilla bean. Use in baked goods and desserts. It's a wonderful addition to hot oatmeal.

There are many more herbs and spices than what I've mentioned here. I encourage you to expand your spice rack to include all of the Lord's wonderful varieties available to us.

*"Better is a dinner of herbs where love is,
than a fatted ox and hatred with it."*

Proverbs 15:17

THE POSITIVE PANTRY

Pasta

~Amaranth–a seed that is high in protein and iron, ground into a powder and added to semolina to make pasta.

~Buckwheat–is said to be one of the best plant protein sources, dark, hardy and flavorful, has a beautiful rich color.

~Corn–corn pasta is usually wheat and gluten free. It is typically made with rice and corn and has a bright yellow color. It cooks fairly quickly, so take care not to overcook.

~Couscous (koos-koos)–made from semolina (ground durum wheat), shaped like little grains.

~Jerusalem artichoke–this artichoke resembles a ginger root. It is pressed, dried and ground into a powder and added to semolina to make pasta; good source of fiber and protein. This is one of my favorite spaghettis.

~Rice–pasta made with brown rice rather than semolina and wheat. It cooks quickly and should be watched while preparing.

~Soba–a dark Japanese noodle made from buckwheat and wheat flour.

~Spinach–pasta made with dried, powdered spinach giving it that dark green color. I love this fettuccine pasta with just a little olive oil, garlic powder and oregano.

~Tomato–pretty orange-colored pasta made with dried tomato powder and semolina.

~100% whole wheat–brown pasta made with 100% whole grain durum wheat.

~Wheat spinach–dark pasta made with whole wheat and spinach powder.

Whole Grains and Rice

~Barley (whole and quick cook)–a good source of fiber. I like to use it in soups and in place of rice. It also makes a lovely hot cereal. Try it in place of oatmeal with a little cinnamon and pure maple syrup or agave nectar.

~Brown basmati rice–this rice has longer grains than most types and tends to be less sticky.

~Bulgur wheat–parboiled, quick cooking wheat, often used in Middle Eastern dishes. This is the main ingredient in my Tabouli recipe.

~Kasha–baked or boiled buckwheat, often found in healthy boxed cereal.

~Long/short grain brown rice–unlike white rice, brown rice has the bran and germ intact, making it rich in vitamins, minerals and fiber. This is the way God intended us to eat it.

~Millet–not just for the birds, this small grass seed is grown all over the world. I make a lovely pudding with millet that is surprisingly yummy.

~Oat bran–the outer layer of the oat, high in fiber and low in fat.

~Quinoa (keen-wah)–a protein rich, grain-like seed, which has a light creamy texture. I've used it in place of rice. The taste is mild enough to go with anything. Try my Quinoa salad!

~Rolled oats–your everyday oats; they have been rolled into flat flakes, steamed and toasted.

~Steel cut oats–not rolled and processed like traditional oatmeal. It is hardy and tasty. It takes more time to prepare and it's deliciously well worth it. I cook mine with raisins; drizzled with a little raw honey.

~Spelt–a grain from the wheat family. It can be substituted for whole wheat in many recipes.

~Whole grain all natural boxed mixes (tabouli, falafel/chickpea meatball, rice pilaf)–these only need a few more ingredients to prepare; great when time is limited. They can be high in sodium, so do not use often.

~Wild rice–actually a grass and not rice, usually domestically grown, not wild, high in protein and fiber and low in fat. It is more expensive than rice and adds a lovely splash of color to any rice dish.

Flour and Mixes

~Barley flour–mild flavored flour made from the barley grain; contains some gluten.

~Oat flour–is easily made by blending rolled oats in a blender until flour consistency. This can be used as a thickener or egg replacement to bind baked goods.

~Rye flour–dark flour made by grinding the whole rye grain; used in rye and pumpernickel breads.

~Sorghum flour–a ground cereal grain much like millet. I like to add it to my baked goods. It turns my banana bread into banana cake. Just replace ½ cup of whole wheat flour with ½ cup of sorghum flour in your recipes.

~Whole grain biscuit, muffin and pancake mix–all natural mix, without aluminum bicarbonate. Be sure to read your labels for the healthiest ingredients.

~Whole grain corn meal–a meal made from corn. Be sure it is not genetically modified (non-GMO).

~White wheat flour–never bleached (food additive added to make it appear whiter) and never bromated (treated with bromic acid)

~Whole wheat pastry flour–ground soft white wheat, lighter flour than whole wheat which works well in baked goods.

~Whole wheat flour–flour made by grinding the entire wheat berry including the bran.

~Yellow corn polenta (grits)–coarsely ground corn. Can be eaten as hot porridge or cooled until firm and sliced and/or reheated. Look for my Polenta pie recipe.

Dried/prepared Beans or Legumes (Most beans are a good source of protein and low in fat)

~Adzuki bean (ah-zoo-kee)–a small red bush bean with a white line on one side. It can be used in almost any bean dish; it sprouts well too.

~Black bean–a small, black bean that is very versatile. I like to add these to salads or bean and rice dishes.

~Black-eyed pea–is actually a bean, creamy tan in color with a distinct black spot (eye) on one side. I like to use these in my bean salad recipe.

~Chick peas (garbanzo beans)–a creamy, yellow round bean with a nutty flavor. This is the main ingredient in my hummus (Arabic word for chickpea) recipe.

~Great northern bean–creamy white in color with a mild flavor.

~Kidney bean–large, dark red color with a distinct kidney shape. Beans are a "meaty" addition to many a meal for us.

~Lentils (red/orange, green, yellow)–a type of pulse or legume, small and round. If you've never tried them, my lentil stew would make a simple and delicious introduction to your palate! They can also be sprouted.

~Lima bean–a light green bean with a meaty texture, often called butter bean because of its buttery taste.

~Mung bean–a small round bean with a medium green color. They are great for sprouting.

~Navy bean–smaller than great northern beans, creamy white in color, similar in taste to great northern beans.

~Pinto bean–when dry it is a speckled brown/red bean. I often use these in Mexican dishes.

~Split peas–bright green dried peas that have been split. These make a quick nutritious soup.

Nuts and Seeds (raw, unsalted, unroasted, no candy coatings- store in refrigerator)

~Alfalfa seed–buy organic seeds for sprouting. They are a healthy addition to any salad.

~Almond–the seed of the almond tree, related to the peach. The inside of the peach pit resembles the almond. You'll need these for my almond milk recipe.

~Brazil nuts–a large white nut with a dark, rough brown shell. Of all other nuts this is among the highest in fat.

~Caraway seed–crescent-shaped seeds with the flavor a bit like anise seed, usually used in rye bread, kraut, curries and German dishes. Add these seeds to my cabbage and noodle recipe.

~Coconut flesh, shredded or flakes–use unsweetened and fresh only. This is a wonderful addition to my apple salad.

~Flax seed (brown or golden)–a small seed about the size of a sesame seed that is plumb packed with healthy benefits, namely healthy fats. I consume ground flax seed every morning.

~Hazel nuts (filberts)–a small ivory-colored nut in a copper-colored shell, with a distinct flavor all its own.

~Pecan–product of the hickory tree family; can be used in a wide variety of baked goods and salads.

~Pignoli or Pine nut–ivory-colored seeds found inside pinecones, sweet and nutty in flavor. They can be on the expensive side. I use these or walnuts in my pesto recipe.

~Poppy seed–tiny, nutty flavored seeds with a black color. They are typically used in cakes and breads.

~Pumpkin seed (pepitas)–flat, dark green, edible seed of the pumpkin. Don't throw away that holiday pumpkin without retrieving the seeds first.

~Sesame seed–a small cream-colored seed with a nutty taste. When they are ground into butter they make tahini.

~Sunflower seed–seed of the beautiful sunflower, gray tear-shaped seeds with a nutty flavor. I like to add these to my homemade raw trail mix.

~Walnut–a brown brain-shaped nut that is adaptable to any recipe that calls for nuts. They taste great in my raw cranberry salad.

Vinegar and Oil

~Balsamic vinegar (preferably sulfite-free)–dark, sweet, syrup-like vinegar. It adds a lovely touch to any vinaigrette.

~Coconut oil–organic, extra virgin is best; can be used in place of butter.

~Extra virgin olive oil–organic is best but very expensive; look for first cold pressed (chemical-free processed at low temperatures) on the label. This is indispensable in my pantry.

~Flax seed oil—yellowish oil made from the flax seed, it has one of the richest sources of omega 3 fatty acid.

~Grape seed oil—pressed from the seeds of various varieties of grapes. It is a great skin moisturizer.

~Raw vinegar (apple cider, red wine)—unpasteurized, unheated vinegar from fermented apples/grapes, no preservatives added.

~Safflower oil—oil from the seeds of the safflower, flavorless, colorless and similar to sunflower oil.

~Walnut oil—medium light oil, popular in salad dressing with a light walnut taste.

Butters and Condiments

~Almond butter—nut butter made from dry roasted or raw almonds. This makes a yummy peanut butter substitute.

~Blackstrap molasses—all natural, unsulphured, a good source of calcium and iron.

~Dried fruit—naturally dehydrated without sulfur dioxide.

~Natural mayonnaise—all natural mayo made from expeller pressed oils and natural ingredients; use sparingly.

~Natural jelly or jam—sweetened with fruit juice instead of sugar or high fructose corn syrup.

~Nutritional yeast flakes—tan yeast flakes grown on beet molasses, naturally rich in vitamins and minerals. It has a cheesy taste.

~Organic raisins—conventionally grown raisins may have a concentrated amount of pesticides.

~Raw unfiltered honey–dark, cloudy honey that is unheated, unpasteurized and unprocessed. I use it as a sugar substitute. It also has wonderful medicinal properties.

~Salsa–a Mexican-style sauce made from tomatoes, mild to very hot in flavor. It is easy to find without harmful ingredients, but raw homemade is best.

~Sesame tahini–nut butter made from dry roasted sesame seeds.

~Sucanat (brand name)–brown, non-refined cane sugar, with a maple-like flavor. This is my favorite dry sugar substitute.

~Tamari sauce–a naturally brewed soy sauce. The organic low sodium variety is best.

~Tomatoes (canned)–organic, low sodium; all natural brands are best. Because each one tastes different, I use several brands of crushed tomatoes for my spaghetti sauce.

Miscellaneous

~Carob powder–comes from the pods of an evergreen tree in the Mediterranean area; it does not contain caffeine, has less fat than cocoa, and is a cocoa powder substitute. Try my carob cake recipe.

~Ezekiel bread (brand name)–sprouted 100% whole grain bread as described in the Holy Scripture (Ezekiel 4:9). It is on the expensive side. This is our favorite bread, hardy and satisfying.

~Herbal tea–caffeine-free, herbal blends found in any supermarket.

~Rice and Almond milk–cow milk replacement found in your local supermarket, used for cereal, to lighten tea and baking. I recommend the non-enriched kind. Homemade is best.

~Teeccino (brand name)–coffee substitute, caffeine-free blend of grain, fruit, herbs and nuts. This is my all-time favorite coffee alternative. My favorite flavor is amaretto.

~Tortillas–whole grain flat rounds, without preservatives. I have yet to find a healthy brand in a regular grocery store. They freeze well and are versatile. I use these in my burrito and tortilla pizza recipes.

~Whole grain boxed cereal–preferably organic, 100% whole grain, low/no sugar. Not all cereals are created equal; many are processed with BHT (food additive). Read your labels. The best boxed cereals are found in health food stores.

~Whole grain bread–baked without preservatives, additives, chemicals or coloring. You can tell when bread is unhealthy, simply by viewing how long the ingredient list is. Homemade bread can be made with as little as 5 ingredients. If you can't read it, don't eat it!

*I am always adding and subtracting various items from my pantry throughout the year. These are just a few staples I keep on hand. A positive pantry = a healthier family!

Health in Season

*Grow your own *Buy organic *Buy local

~April

Asparagus, banana, cabbage, escarole (variety of endive lettuce, lovely prepared with minced garlic and olive oil), onion, pineapple, radish, rhubarb (looks like red celery, usually used in dessert recipes), spinach, strawberry (Find a local u-pick farm this month.)

~May

Asparagus, banana, celery, papaya (a large oblong-shaped fruit loaded with beneficial enzymes; often green in the store; ripen at room temperature to a golden orange), peas, pineapple, potato, strawberry, tomato (grow your own easily and save $), watercress (peppery tasting, leafy herb from the mustard family)

~June

Apricot, avocado (dark green, pear-shaped fruit, not sweet, creamy and loaded with good fat; add some to your salad or veggie sandwich for a meaty texture), banana, cantaloupe, cherries, corn, cucumber, figs (typically found dried, but they are delicious raw), green beans, lime, mango (scrumptious oval-shaped fruit with peach-colored flesh; seed resembles a bird's cuttlebone), nectarine, onion, peaches, peas, peppers, pineapple, plum

~July

Apricots, banana, blueberry (find a local u-pick this month), cabbage, cantaloupe, cherries, corn, cucumbers, dill, eggplant (a dark, purple-black colored, pear-shaped veggie; peel and cube some into your next spaghetti sauce), figs, green beans, nectarines, okra (a fuzzy, green pod veggie; tastes lovely raw too), peaches (find a local u-pick farm this month), peppers, watermelon (It is no coincidence that this water-filled fruit grows during the hot months when we need it the most.)

~August

Apples (u-pick), banana, beets, various berries (u-pick), cabbage, carrots, corn, cucumber, eggplant, figs, melon, nectarines, peaches, pears, peppers, plums, potato, summer squash (zucchini, yellow squash), tomato

~September

Apples, banana, broccoli, carrots, cauliflower, corn, cucumber, grapes, greens (kale, mustard, collards, lettuces), melon, okra, onion, potato, summer squash, yams (similar to sweet potato)

~October

Apples, banana, broccoli, grapes, peppers, persimmons (dark orange fruit that looks similar to tomato), pumpkin (retrieve those seeds), yams

~November

Apples, banana, broccoli, cabbage, cauliflower, cranberries (freezes well; stock up while in season), dates, eggplant, mushrooms, pumpkin, sweet potato

~December

Apples, avocado, banana, grapefruit, lemon, lime (Isn't it neat how the Lord supplies us with citrus fruits rich in vitamin C, during the cold and flu season?) mushrooms, oranges, pears, pineapple, tangerine, pomegranate (looks like a large cranberry with hundreds of pulpy seeds inside; don't be afraid to try these, they're delicious)

Yet He did not neglect to leave some witness of Himself, for He did you good and (showed you) kindness and gave you rains from heaven and fruitful seasons, satisfying your hearts with nourishment and happiness

Acts 14:17

HEALTHY SUBSTITUTIONS

Black pepper–1 tsp black pepper = $1/8$ tsp cayenne pepper

Bread crumbs–toasted 100% all natural whole grain bread processed into crumbs, toasted oatmeal, or crushed all natural whole grain cereal

Butter (buy organic, use sparingly)–to grease a pan use olive, safflower, sunflower or grape seed oil. A drizzle of olive oil on a baked potato is yummy.

Shortening or lard–substitute ½ cup all natural apple sauce (unsweetened) for 1 cup shortening

Buttermilk–1 cup = 1 cup rice/almond milk minus 1 Tbsp, plus 1 Tbsp fresh lemon or lime juice

Chips–baked all natural store bought chips or my baked chip recipe

Chocolate chips–vegetarian carob chips (found in your local health food store)

Cocoa powder–1 cup cocoa powder = 1 cup carob powder

Corn starch–1 Tbsp = 1 Tbsp arrowroot powder

Currents–raisins, chopped dates, figs, dehydrated fruits like pineapple, papaya, apple or apricot (no sulfur dioxide)

Eggs - one egg = 2 Tbsp oat flour or half of a mashed banana or ¼ cup quick cook oatmeal or ¼ cup ground flax seed or ¼ cup psyllium husk powder

Flour–if a recipe calls for 2 cups of all-purpose white flour, substitute any combination of healthier flour; 1 cup whole wheat and 1 cup pastry flour or 1 cup sorghum flour and 1 cup white wheat flour

Garlic–1 medium clove = 1 tsp minced garlic or ¼ tsp granulated garlic

Lemon juice/zest–lime or orange juice/zest

Meat–all natural veggie burgers, bulgur wheat, beans, lentils

Milk–1 cup = 1 cup almond or rice milk

Peanut butter–(peanuts are hard to digest) 1 cup = 1 cup almond butter; ¾ cup tahini or sunflower butter

Pumpkin puree–banana, prepared sweet potato or yams

Store bought juice–freshly extracted raw juice

Sugar, brown–1 cup = ½ cup Sucanat (brand name) and 1 Tbsp blackstrap molasses (unsulphured)

Sugar, white–1 cup = ½ cup Sucanat (brand name); ½ cup pure maple syrup; ½ cup raw honey; ⅔ cup rice syrup (sweetener made from brown rice); ½ cup agave nectar; 1 tsp stevia (a sweet herb grown in S. America; much sweeter than sugar, use it sparingly) or ⅔ cup mashed over-ripe banana.

White rice–1 cup = 1 cup brown rice; 1 cup whole barley or any variety of grain

White flour tortilla–all natural whole grain tortilla; my homemade crepe recipe.

*Do not throw away your old recipe books; simply replace unhealthy ingredients with healthier ones.

NewTrishUs Recipes

~Main Dishes~

Spaghetti Sauce

2 cans crushed tomatoes (28 oz.) use 2 different brands with low sodium
4 cloves minced garlic
2 Tbsp basil
3 Tbsp oregano
1 Tbsp parsley flakes
1 large or 2 small bay leaf
*add mushrooms, green pepper, zucchini or eggplant for variations.

Cook on low/med heat for approximately 1 hour until thick and darker red. Stir in 3 Tbsp of extra virgin olive oil before serving. For a spicy sauce add 1 Tbsp pizza peppers while cooking. Serve over any whole grain pasta, cooked al dente' (firm but not hard). You can also use this on pizza or inside a baked potato. *Buon appetito*!

SIMPLE BASIL PASTA

Boil any shape whole grain pasta el dente'. Drizzle pasta with extra virgin olive oil. Add garlic powder or fresh minced garlic (even better), a pinch of natural sea salt and ground basil or oregano to taste. Mix and enjoy!

PESTO

1 packed cup of fresh basil leaves
1/3 cup pine nuts or walnuts
3 cloves garlic
Extra virgin olive oil

Process everything in a food processor using the S blade. Drizzle in oil while processing until a smooth paste forms. Add natural sea salt to taste. Serve over whole grain pasta, grains, baked potato, in place of mayonnaise on a wrap or tossed into any veggie dish.

STUFFED AUBERGINE (EGGPLANT)

2 large eggplants washed
2 celery stalks chopped
1 large green pepper diced
1 medium onion diced

2 garlic cloves minced

1 tsp rinsed capers (picked immature buds of the caper bush) – optional

½ cup pine nuts or chopped walnuts

1 tsp natural sea salt

1 tsp oregano

1 tsp basil

1 can diced tomato (15 oz) drained well

Poke all around the eggplant with a fork and bake in a 450° oven for 20 minutes. Set aside to cool. Sauté the celery, green pepper, onion, garlic, capers, nuts, salt and spices. Cut the cooled eggplant in half the long way and scoop away the flesh, leaving enough to hold its shape. Chop the eggplant insides into small chunks and add it to the sautéed veggies. Add the tomato and cook until all the veggies are tender. Stuff the eggplant shells full and heat through for 15-20 minutes in a 350° oven. Drizzle with extra virgin olive oil before serving.

Polenta Pie

3 cups low/no sodium vegetable broth or pure water

1 cup polenta (coarse cornmeal)

4 Tbsp fresh herbs (sage, basil, oregano, dill, chives)

1½ tsp natural sea salt

2 large garlic cloves minced

Fresh tomato thinly sliced into rounds

Boil broth or water in a large sauce pan; gradually stir in the polenta. Watch and stir over med/low heat for approximately 25 minutes or until the polenta is done. Be careful, the thickened polenta pops and splatters. Stir in herbs, garlic and salt. Spoon polenta evenly into a lightly olive oiled glass pie dish. Spread the fresh tomato over the polenta and press them down into it a bit. Cool and cut into pie slices. This makes a lovely substitute for bread/rolls with a meal.

Veggie Wraps

Spread a whole-grain tortilla with hummus, *guacamole or pesto. Add finely chopped cucumber, tomatoes, red onion, spinach, black olives, shredded lettuce and artichoke hearts. Fold and enjoy. You can use any raw veggies you have on hand. *Look for my homemade recipes.

Simple Tortilla Pizzas

Using all natural tortillas for the crust, spread prepared spaghetti sauce or pesto on top. Sprinkle with any variety of pizza toppings you desire (mushrooms, olives, onion, artichoke hearts, fresh tomato, spinach, pizza peppers). Heat until warmed through. Each tortilla makes an individual-size pizza. With all of those toppings, you won't even miss the cheese!

Bean Burritos

2 cans beans rinsed and drained (black, pinto or kidney) or 2 cups prepared dry beans
¼ cup chopped onion
1 tsp cumin
½ tsp hot pepper sauce (optional)
Pkg. 6 whole-grain tortillas
Finely chopped green pepper, onion, tomato, black olives
1 large can crushed tomatoes or salsa

Coat a 9 × 13" pan with ½ of the canned tomato or salsa to keep the burritos from sticking. In your food processor process beans, ¼ cup onion, cumin and hot sauce until smooth. If this mixture is too stiff, you can add water or salsa to thin it a bit. Spoon out equally onto the tortillas in a long mound. Sprinkle each with the chopped veggies. Roll the burritos loosely taking care not to squish out the filling. Place in pan and cover with the remaining tomatoes or salsa. Cover and heat through in a 350° oven for approximately 15-20 minutes. *You may like to add my bulgur wheat taco *meat* to this recipe.

Mock Tuna

1 cup raw almonds soaked in pure water for 8* or more hours; drain well
1 small onion
1 celery stalk
All natural mayonnaise, natural sea salt and kelp powder (optional) to taste

Process almonds in food processor with *S* blade until grainy/powdery texture. Place in mixing bowl. Process celery and onion until minced, add to bowl. Add mayo and natural sea salt to your liking. Add kelp powder to intensify that *tuna* taste. Serve with whole grain crackers or bread. You can even use this for a raw veggie dip if you like.

*The soaking process rinses off the enzyme inhibitors naturally found in nuts.

POTATO SOUP

3 pounds potatoes (organic is best)
1 large onion chopped
5 cloves garlic chopped
1 large bay leaf
Natural sea salt

Peel and cube potatoes. Boil in purified water with onion and garlic as if you were making mashed potatoes. When the vegetables are soft, mash them with an immersion hand blender until smooth and creamy. Add more or less water depending on the consistency you prefer. Add the bay leaf and salt to taste. Cook for 5 minutes more so the bay leaf permeates the soup. Stir well and serve hot. Add broccoli until softened and blend for broccoli soup or mushrooms for mushroom soup, cauliflower, asparagus or spinach. Just use the potato soup as your base. The possibilities are endless!

Lentil Stew

1 bag of dried lentils (16 oz.) or 2 cups

7 cups purified water

1 28 oz. can low sodium (organic) crushed tomatoes

5 cloves minced garlic

1 large onion chopped

3 Tbsp Italian seasoning

1 large bay leaf

2 tsp pizza peppers (optional)

Natural sea salt

3 Tbsp extra virgin olive oil

Sort through lentils for any stones and rinse well. Place lentils in a large soup pot with water, crushed tomato, garlic, onion and spices. Simmer gently until lentils are tender, approximately 20-25 minutes; stir occasionally. Add more water if you like a thinner stew. Add salt to taste. Before serving, mix in 3 Tbsp olive oil. Carrot rounds or potato cubes can be added to this stew for a different variation. This soup can be made ahead or frozen for busy days.

French Onion Soup

Fill a large soup pot ⅓ full with chopped onion; sauté and brown in a little water or vegetable broth and 2 tsp extra virgin olive oil for approximately 30 minutes. The browning takes some time. You'll want to caramelize the onion. The pot should have brown bits on the bottom. Be careful not to burn the onion. When you've reached this point, add enough pure water or vegetable stock to make the soup your desired consistency. Add a large bay leaf, 1 Tbsp of parsley and heat through for 10 more minutes. Add salt to taste. This would taste lovely with my garlic toast croutons on top.

BULGUR TACO *MEAT*

1 cup bulgur wheat
¾ cup pureed tomato
¾ cup pure water
1 tsp cumin
½ tsp natural sea salt
¼ tsp chili powder

Mix bulgur wheat, cumin, chili powder and salt in a bowl. In a sauce pot stir together tomato puree and water; bring to a boil. Pour boiled mixture over the wheat, stir and cover for approximately 30 minutes or until the wheat is tender. Stir and use anywhere you'd use taco meat–burritos, taco salad or stuffed peppers.

EGGPLANT BURGERS

Wash eggplant well. Cut into ½" rounds. Sprinkle both sides with dried basil, oregano and natural sea salt. Place on an olive oil or coconut oil coated broiler pan. Broil on medium until eggplant is tender and brown, turning once. Keep a close eye on them so they don't burn. Serve with onion and tomato just like a burger. You can also make portabella mushroom burgers the same way. For a different variation marinate them in Italian vinaigrette first.

Stuffed Peppers

2 Bell peppers (green, red, yellow or even poblano)
1 medium onion diced
3 garlic cloves minced
3 Tbsp pure water or vegetable stock
Prepared taco *meat* recipe
1 cup pure water
Extra virgin olive oil

Wash and core peppers, taking care to keep them whole for stuffing. Sauté onion and garlic in 3 Tbsp of water or vegetable stock until tender. Stir in the prepared taco *meat*. Add extra seasoning to your desired taste, (cumin, hot sauce, salt). Stuff peppers full, careful not to split them. Stand them up in a baking dish; add water to the bottom of the dish. Lightly drizzle pepper tops with extra virgin olive oil. Cover and bake 350°, for approximately 1 hour or until peppers are tender. Substitute Mexican spices for Italian ones and serve with my spaghetti sauce for a tasty change.

Pizza Salad

~Crust
1 cup whole wheat bread flour
1 cup whole grain spelt or white wheat or a combo of both
1 tsp active dry yeast
1 Tbsp extra virgin olive oil
2/3 cup warm pure water
Corn meal

~Crust topping
2-3 large garlic cloves minced
1 Tbsp extra virgin olive oil
Pinch of natural sea salt
Sesame, caraway seeds, oregano, Italian seasoning, crushed red pizza peppers (optional)

Place the first 5 ingredients in a bread machine (follow bread-maker instructions for dough) or make by hand. When dough is done, oil and dust 14″ non-aluminum pan with cornmeal. Roll out the dough onto the pan. Mix the garlic, oil and salt and spread over the dough evenly. Sprinkle with any combination of spices and seeds that you desire. Bake in a 350° oven for 15-20 minutes. Cool to lukewarm.

~Salad

Use any variety of lettuce and veggies you have on hand. Also I like to add all natural olives, artichoke hearts and fresh mushrooms.

Cut pizza crust into 8 triangles. Place 2 slices on a dinner plate; top with salad and pour your favorite salad dressing on top. I like to use Italian vinaigrette because it soaks down into the crust.

CABBAGE AND NOODLES

In a large pot, sauté a 2 pound head of shredded cabbage, 2 large chopped onions and 4 large minced garlic cloves in ½ cup of pure water or vegetable stock. Cook down until soft and a little brown. Meanwhile prepare a package of all natural whole grain noodles. Stir the noodles into the cooked cabbage. Add natural sea salt to taste, lightly coat with extra virgin olive oil, stir well. A Tbsp of caraway seeds gives this dish a tasty zing.

Curried Lentils

1 large onion chopped
¼ cup pure water or vegetable stock
2 large garlic cloves minced
1 cup chopped fresh tomato
1 bay leaf
3 cardamom seeds
1 tsp natural sea salt
1½ Tbsp curry powder
¼ tsp cayenne pepper powder (optional)
3 cups prepared green lentils

Sauté the onion and garlic in water until tender. Add fresh tomato, bay leaf, cardamom, salt, curry and cayenne powder. Cook for approximately 5 minutes, so that the spices release their flavors into the veggies. Mix in the lentils and continue to heat through. Remove bay leaf and all 3 cardamom seeds. This may be served on its own over rice or with any grain. Substitute a medley of mixed veggies for the lentils for another variation.

Flat Tacos

Small 6" all natural corn tortillas
2 cans organic pinto beans drained
1 tsp cumin
Shredded lettuce
Chopped black olives
Chopped tomatoes
Raw corn

Sliced avocado or homemade guacamole
Raw salsa (or all-natural store bought salsa)
Any variety of finely chopped veggies

Spread tortillas out on a flat cookie sheet; toast in a 350° oven until crisp (Be careful! They burn easily.) Mash the beans and cumin with a potato masher. Set out all of the ingredients on the table/counter-top and have the family/guests build their own flat tacos. Start with a layer of beans and layer up from there. Half the fun is building your own.

Lentil Loaf

1 small onion
1 large garlic clove
¼ cup rolled oats (oatmeal)
½ cup bread crumbs (process 1 or 2 slices of whole grain bread in food-processor)
½ tsp ground thyme
1 tsp natural sea salt or 2 tsp tamari
2 Tbsp ground flax seed mixed with 1 Tbsp pure water
4 cups cooked green lentils

In a food processor using the S blade, process onion, garlic, bread crumbs, flax seed, oats, thyme and salt until finely chopped. Gradually add the lentils until it has dough like consistency. Olive oil a glass loaf pan well. Press the lentil mixture into the loaf pan; spread on a layer of all-natural ketchup if desired. Bake 350° for 45 minutes. Let set for 10 minutes before slicing. The longer you wait, the firmer it gets. Enjoy hot or cool completely and slice to make lentil loaf sandwiches. I like mine with mayo, raw onion, salt and pepper.

MEXICAN POTATO CASSEROLE

Slice into thin rounds 2 pounds of unpeeled potatoes (I use russet but any variety will do). A food processor will make this job quicker and the potatoes will be sliced thin and even. In a 9 × 13" pan pour a thin layer of canned crushed tomatoes. Place one layer of potato, corn, black beans and thinly sliced onion in pan. Pour all natural spicy salsa in a thin layer on top. Repeat with a layer of potato, corn, black beans, onion and salsa. If you run out of salsa use the rest of the crushed tomato. You may add any Mexican type spice/ingredients you wish to this dish (black olives, jalapenos, green peppers, cumin, and oregano). Bake covered 350°, for 45-50 minutes or until the potatoes are fork tender.

GLUTEN *WHEAT BALLS*

1 cup vital wheat gluten
½ cup whole wheat flour
1 tsp parsley
1 tsp chopped onion flake
1 tsp garlic powder
½ tsp natural sea salt
1 tsp oregano
1 cup pure cold water
Large pot of pure boiling water

Mix dry ingredients thoroughly. Add water; knead until elastic feeling is obtained. Roll into tsp size balls. Drop into boiling water for 20 minutes. Reduce heat, to keep the wheat ball from breaking apart. Drain in colander. Preheat oven 350°. Lightly coat wheat balls in extra virgin olive oil.

Cook on lightly oiled cookie sheet for 25 minutes turning a few times to brown evenly. Let set for 5 minutes before serving. Serve with spaghetti sauce–adding to sauce right before serving; meat ball hero; with hummus in whole grain pita pocket; dip into my homemade BBQ sauce; or add to wraps.

STUFFED POTATO

In a bowl place shredded zucchini (or any veggie you prefer), finely chopped onion, celery, cucumber, diced tomato and minced garlic (Be sure the veggies are chopped fine.) Stir in extra virgin olive oil, natural sea salt, oregano, basil and parsley to taste (Fresh herbs would make it even tastier.) Bake large russet potato until soft; cut in half; score flesh (so the veggie dressing can absorb down into it), and pile on the raw veggie topping. Place this same mixture over prepared whole grain pasta, grains or brown rice for a healthy change.

~Salads~

Salad bar Night

- Lettuce base–raw spinach, romaine, green and red leaf lettuce, spring mix, bib lettuce

- Variety of diced veggies–broccoli, zucchini, cucumber, celery, onion, beet, tomato, radish, yellow squash, carrots, bell pepper, raw corn, shredded purple or green cabbage, cauliflower, mushrooms, sprouts

- Cooked and cooled grains–barley, brown rice, quinoa, millet

- Beans–garbanzo, kidney, black-eyed peas, great northern, pinto, black

- Raw seeds–sunflower, sesame, pumpkin, flax

- Fresh herbs–oregano, basil, parsley, chives, dill, mint

- Toppings–olives, grapes, orange sections, artichoke hearts, garlic toast croutons avocado. Squeeze fresh lemon juice over the avocado to keep it from turning brown (oxidation).

Display items in individual containers on your countertop or table, along with an assortment of dressings. Enjoy a salad bar at home.

RAW CRANBERRY SALAD

1 lb bag raw cranberries

1 organic orange, washed and unpeeled

1 organic apple cored (sweet variety)

½ cup chopped walnuts

¼ cup honey, agave or Sucanat (brand name) sugar

Sort and wash cranberries well, careful to remove rotten/soft ones. In a food processor, process cranberries into small coarse pieces; place in a large mixing bowl. Process apple and orange into a chunky applesauce consistency; mix with cranberries. Add walnuts and sweetener and mix well. To enjoy this dish longer, purchase cranberries while in season and freeze.

BUILD A BEAN SALAD

In a large bowl add any variety of organic, low sodium canned beans (drained and rinsed), or any variety of prepared dried beans. I use a combination of black, pinto, kidney, garbanzo, navy and black-eyed pea. Place diced onion, cucumber, tomato or any diced raw veggies you prefer into separate containers. Left-over cold whole grain pasta or brown rice would go well with this too. I usually set this out in a salad bar fashion so folks can choose what they like. Top this salad with my *NewTrishUs* vinaigrette or any healthy dressing you enjoy.

PASTA SALAD

Boil any variety of whole grain pasta; cool. Rub a sliced raw garlic clove around the inside of a large bowl, add finely chopped cucumber, onion, tomato, natural olives, celery, zucchini, broccoli or any chopped raw veggies you have on hand. Toss in my *NewTrishUs* vinaigrette before serving and enjoy. This is a quick and easy meal to make especially if you have left-over pasta.

POTATO SALAD

2 pounds potato

$1/3$ cup all natural mayonnaise

1 Tbsp yellow mustard

1 tsp garlic powder

1 tsp natural sea salt

1 tsp Dijon mustard

1 tsp paprika

1 Tbsp dried parsley flakes (fresh is even better)

½ cup chopped onion or green onion

1 Tbsp chopped fresh chives (optional)

Pierce each potato with a fork once on each side, boil with skin on (in pure water) until soft but not mushy (the skin helps keep potato from breaking apart). Cool and peel by hand. Thin-skin potatoes like red or new potatoes can keep their skins on. Cut potatoes into ½" chunks. In a large bowl mix together all other ingredient, add potato, mix well and chill.

Bulgur Tabouli Salad

1 cup bulgur wheat
1½ cup boiling purified water
1 tsp all natural sea salt
¼ cup fresh lemon juice
4 Tbsp extra virgin olive oil
2 medium garlic cloves minced
1 large tomato diced
2 cups fresh parsley chopped (Dried parsley will not work in this recipe.)
1 small onion chopped fine

In a large bowl (not plastic) pour boiling water over wheat, cover and let sit for 30 minutes. Chill wheat. Add the rest of the ingredients, mix well and enjoy. This is a traditional version of tabouli salad, but you can add other fresh veggies like mushrooms or green and red bell pepper. Try using quinoa in place of the wheat for a different variation (1 cup quinoa to 2 cups pure water; simmer low for 25 minutes or until tender).

Brown Rice Salad

2 cups cooked brown rice, cooled
1 cup green, yellow and red diced bell pepper
¼ cup diced onion
½ cup diced tomato
½ tsp natural sea salt
1 large garlic clove minced
3 Tbsp fresh dill
¼ cup fresh parsley chopped

¹/₃ cup fresh lemon juice
¼ cup extra virgin olive oil
1 Tbsp Dijon mustard

Add rice and veggies to mixing bowl. In a mason jar shake up the rest of the ingredients for a dressing. Add dressing before serving.

Black Bean Corn Salad

Place approximately 2 cups fresh raw corn off the cob or frozen organic sweet white or yellow corn (thawed) in a mixing bowl. Add 1 can of black beans drained and rinsed or 1 cup prepared dried black beans. Mix in 1 large garlic clove minced and ½ cup each diced tomato, green bell pepper and onion. Add ¼ cup of your favorite all natural salsa and chili powder to taste. Mix well, chill and enjoy!

Raw Slaw

In a large bowl mix together 4 cups shredded cabbage, 1 cup shredded carrot, ½ cup finely chopped celery, ½ tsp dill, 1 large garlic clove minced, ½ tsp natural sea salt (optional), 2 Tbsp raw honey and ½ cup natural mayo. Mix well and chill.

APPLE SALAD

Combine 4 cups cubed raw sweet apples, 2 stalks celery diced, ½ cup chopped raw walnuts and ½ cup organic black raisins. Mix in enough natural mayo to coat lightly. Chill and serve. Add a cup of halved grapes for a different twist.

QUINOA SALAD

1 cup quinoa
2 cups pure water
2 cups finely chopped veggies (celery, onion, zucchini, cucumber, bell pepper)
¼ cup extra virgin olive oil
¼ cup fresh lemon juice
1 tsp basil
2 cloves garlic minced
½ tsp natural sea salt

In a pot bring water to a boil, add quinoa. Reduce heat, cover and simmer 25 minutes until liquid is absorbed, cool. Add veggies and cooled quinoa to salad bowl. In a jar mix the rest of the ingredients. Add dressing before serving; mix well. This serves nicely on a bed of lettuce with tomato wedges.

AMBROSIA

In a large bowl place 5 peeled, seeded and cubed oranges, 4 cored and diced sweet apples, 1 cup diced fresh pineapple, 2 large firm bananas cut into ½" rounds. Mix in gently, ¼ cup shredded unsweetened coconut and ½ cup chopped raw walnuts. In a food processor add ½ cup shredded unsweetened coconut, 6 pitted dates and enough purified water to make a paste-like dressing for the fruit. Mix dressing into the fruit and enjoy.

CARROT SALAD

Peel and shred 2 pounds raw carrots in a food processor. Mix in 2 cups fresh cubed pineapple, ½ cup organic raisins and ½ cup chopped raw walnuts. In a blender blend ½ cup pineapple chunks, 3 pitted dates and ¼ cup chopped raw walnuts to make a dressing. Add dressing to carrot salad and mix well.

APPLE PEAR DATE SALAD

1 sweet apple cored and diced
2 pears cored and diced
¾ cup dates chopped
1 cup chopped celery
½ cup chopped raw walnuts
¼ cup all natural mayonnaise

1 Tbsp raw honey

1 Tbsp fresh lemon juice

1 tsp grated lemon peel (organic)

Toss diced fruit with celery and nuts. Combine remaining ingredients and toss with fruit. Chill and serve.

Raw Veggie Salad

In a mixing bowl add any assortment of finely chopped veggies (purple or green cabbage, bell pepper, celery, carrot, onion, tomato, zucchini, yellow squash, cauliflower, and broccoli). The key is to chop them into *very* small pieces. I've found that raw vegetable salads are much more enjoyable this way. Add my *NewTrishus* Italian vinaigrette and marinate for 2 hours, stirring occasionally.

NewTrishUs Italian Vinaigrette

¼ cup first cold pressed extra virgin olive oil

⅔ cup raw wine vinegar

½ cup pure water

2 Tbsp Dijon mustard

1 Tbsp raw honey

1 Tbsp garlic powder

2 tsp paprika

1 heaping Tbsp oregano

2 Tbsp balsamic vinegar (optional)

1 tsp natural sea salt

In a large mason jar, shake all ingredients together well until the honey is dissolved. Store in refrigerator. Olive oil will solidify; remove from refrigerator for approximately 10-15 minutes before serving. I have to admit, this was a difficult recipe to write. Like Mom, I usually don't measure, I just eyeball it.

Ranch Veggie Dip or Dressing

Combine ½ cup all natural mayonnaise, 1½ tsp garlic powder, 1 tsp oregano, 1½ tsp Dijon mustard, mix well and store in a sealed container. Thin with pure water or lemon juice for salad dressing.

Tamari-Ginger Dressing

1 cup first cold pressed extra virgin olive oil

½ cup raw wine or apple cider vinegar

2 Tbsp tamari low sodium organic soy sauce

2 garlic cloves

1" cube of fresh ginger or ½ tsp powdered ginger

2 Tbsp pure water

Place all ingredients except olive oil in a blender; mix well so that the fresh ginger and garlic are pulverized. While the blender is running, slowly add the oil until thick and creamy. Refrigerate in a glass jar. This dressing tastes lovely on my Pizza Salad.

~Side Dishes~

Oven Baked Fries

Cut any variety of potato into wedges, leaving skins on. Place potatoes on a non-aluminum baking sheet skin sides down. This keeps you from using high heated oil. If you lay them on the cut side they will stick without oil. Sprinkle potatoes with garlic powder, oregano, onion powder or any combinations of spices you'd like. Bake at 350° for 45 minutes or until fork tender. This is a fun finger food for the kids to dunk into salsa or all natural ketchup.

Holiday Stuffing

1 loaf of all natural whole grain bread, toasted until crispy

1 large onion diced

3 ribs of celery diced

2 Tbsp extra virgin olive oil

4 cups of all natural unsalted vegetable broth (approximately)

1 tsp powdered thyme

1 tsp sage

1 tsp oregano

(Or substitute 1 rounded Tbsp Italian seasoning for the 3 spices above)

1 tsp natural sea salt

In a large pot sauté onion, celery, salt and spices in oil until tender. Break up toast into 1″ pieces; add to pot, and mix well. Slowly add vegetable broth to lightly moisten toasted bread. Taste to see if there is enough spice. Pour into oiled casserole dish. Cover, bake in 350° oven until heated through. This can be made days in advance, just refrigerate. Serve with my vegetable gravy and raw cranberry salad during the holidays.

RAISIN RICE

2 cups brown rice
3¾ cup pure water
½ cup organic raisins
2 large garlic cloves minced
2 tsp cinnamon
1 tsp nutmeg
¼ tsp natural sea salt
2 Tbsp extra virgin olive oil

Combine all ingredients except the oil in a medium sauce pan; bring to a boil. Stir and reduce heat to low. Cover and cook for approximately 30 minutes or until rice is tender. Stir in oil before serving.

Holiday Sweet Potatoes

Peel and cube 4 large sweet potatoes; boil in pure water until soft enough to mash or pierce and bake at 400° for approximately 1 hour. Drain/peel and mash until smooth. Mix 2 Tbsp cinnamon and 2 Tbsp pure vanilla extract. Spoon into an oiled casserole or loaf pan. Mix together 1 cup chopped pecans, 3 Tbsp raw honey, 1 Tbsp cinnamon and 1 Tbsp pure vanilla; top potatoes with nut mixture. Cover loosely with foil and bake for 25-30 minutes at 350°. I like robust flavors. You may like to adjust the vanilla and cinnamon according to your taste.

~Snacks~

Lime Apple Snack

Core and cut into eighths any sweet variety of apple; place in a bowl. Squeeze ¼ of a large fresh lime over all. The taste of this reminds me of the lemon Italian ice I used to get from the ice cream truck as a kid. Quick, easy and refreshingly delicious.

Raw Nut Bars

In a food processor grind together raw nuts and seeds of any kind into a coarse powder; moisten with honey, agave nectar or pure maple syrup while processing. It should start to form a ball. Add enough oatmeal to form stiff dough. Press into a brownie type pan. Cool in refrigerator until firm. Cut into squares. For different variations try adding raisins, dried (sulphur dioxide free) fruit, shredded unsweetened coconut, or mashed banana. Enjoy!

RAW SALSA AND BAKED CHIPS

Using a circular pizza cutter, cut 100%, all natural corn tortillas into triangles; bake 250° until crisp, careful to watch them so they don't burn. Process together in a food processor fresh tomato, green pepper, onion, garlic, fresh cilantro and hot pepper such as jalapeno, to taste. Refrigerate; flavors will intensify the next day. I make my own chips because foods go through unhealthy chemical changes when oils are subjected to high heat; omit all fried foods for a healthy diet.

RAW TRAIL MIX

Mix together any variety of raw seeds—sesame, sunflower, pumpkin, flax; any variety of raw nuts—almonds, walnuts, pine, pecans, hazel; any variety of dried fruit (no sulfur dioxide)—raisins, apple, apricot, pineapple (not sugar coated), cranberry; any variety of whole grain flakes—rye, oat, barley, wheat. Mix everything together and store in an airtight container in the refrigerator. Seeds and nuts should be unsalted and unroasted. Although they are a good source of healthy fats, eat them as snacks in moderation. My husband likes to keep a container in his desk drawer at work.

Cheesy Popcorn

Pop organic popcorn in a hot air popper; sprinkle on nutritional yeast flakes and natural sea salt to taste (optional). The yeast flakes give the popcorn a cheesy taste. Try garlic or chili powder for popcorn with a kick. Look for popcorn that is not genetically modified.

Simple Banana Snack

Slice a banana or two into a single serve bowl; sprinkle with chopped raw almonds or walnuts, ground flax seed and unsweetened coconut flakes. Drizzle with agave nectar or raw unfiltered honey and enjoy. This can be made with any fruit and nut combo you desire or try my simple carob sauce instead of honey for a guilt-free treat.

Guacamole

2 ripe avocados
1 small tomato
1 small onion
2 Tbsp fresh lemon juice
Natural sea salt to taste (optional)

Process in food processor all ingredients until smooth. Enjoy these with my baked chips, veggies or as a spread for sandwiches. Hard green avocados ripen easily in a few days on the kitchen counter.

Banana on a Stick

Peel a banana, cut in half and push a chop stick or popsicle-type stick into the cut end, freeze. The consistency will get fudgesicle-like, cool and refreshing. These are great for a teething child to suck on. You can also roll the banana in my carob sauce, chopped nuts or unsweetened coconut before freezing.

Smoothies

Blend together any variety of fruit with pure water until smooth. Add frozen fruit or ice for a frostier consistency. If you like it sweeter than the fruits deliver, add raw honey, maple syrup, agave nectar, dates or natural fruit jam sparingly. I like to add a handful of raw spinach or baby carrots to mine; with all the sweet fruits you don't even taste the veggies.

~Desserts~

Black Banana Bread

1½ cup black (over-ripe) banana
¼ cup Sucanat (brand name) sugar or honey
½ cup unsweetened apple sauce
2 Tbsp ground flax seed
2 cups whole grain flour (I use whole wheat, sorghum, white wheat combo)
½ cup chopped nuts or raisins
1 tsp baking soda
2 tsp all natural vanilla extract
½ tsp baking powder (non-aluminum)
Pinch of natural sea salt (optional)

Heat oven to 325°; olive oil and flour a glass or ceramic loaf pan. Mix together sugar, banana, applesauce, and flax seed in a large mixing bowl. Stir in remaining ingredients; pour into prepared pan. Bake for 1 hour or until knife comes out clean. Cool 10 minutes; loosen sides from pan and remove. Let cool completely before slicing. Use prepared pumpkin or sweet potato in place of banana for a delicious alternative.

RAW CAROB PUDDING

Process ripe avocados in food processor until smooth. Add carob powder until dark like chocolate. Slowly drizzle in agave nectar or honey while processing until you achieve the desired sweetness. Tastes often, don't over-sweeten. Cool in refrigerator or consume right away. This is surprisingly delicious and a satisfying healthy alternative.

FRUIT CREPES

Thin out the batter of all natural pancake/waffle mix (some call for egg or oil but I just use pure water). Make a crepe; a large thin pancake on your prepared cast iron or stainless steel pan. Thinly spread with any flavor of natural fruit jam and your choice of sliced fresh fruit, roll up, drizzle with my simple carob sauce or agave nectar and shredded unsweetened coconut and serve.

JUICE POPS

Purchase a juice pop mold at any store (preferably BPA free). Fill each opening with 100% juice (no fructose corn syrup, sugar, artificial sweetener, coloring or preservatives); freeze. You can add sliced banana or grapes before freezing for a fruity twist. Try orange juice and rice/almond milk for a creamsicle-type pop or carob powder blended into rice/almond milk for a fudgesicle-type pop.

Simple Carob Sauce

Place ½ cup of carob powder into a bowl; add enough raw honey, agave nectar or maple syrup to make a chocolate syrup consistency.

Rice Pudding

3 cups cooked cooled brown rice
⅔ cup rice milk, almond milk or water
6 pitted dates or ¼ cup raisins
½ cup unsweetened coconut flakes
1½ tsp pure vanilla
½ tsp cinnamon

Mix the rice with vanilla and cinnamon; set aside. Blend together milk/water with dates/raisins and coconut until smooth and creamy. Add more milk/water if too thick; add to rice; mix well. You may like to mix in ¼ cup raisins, currants, dried apple, dried apricot, or chopped nuts/dates. Chill in refrigerator for at least one hour.

Hearty Lemon Sesame Bread

1 Tbsp baking powder
½ cup raw sunflower seeds
½ cup organic raisins
½ cup almond or rice milk

½ tsp natural sea salt (optional)

⅓ cup unsweetened applesauce

2 cups whole wheat flour

2 Tbsp flax seed

⅓ cup pure water

2 Tbsp sesame seed

3 Tbsp tahini

½ cup Sucanat (brand name) sugar

*Juice and peel of 1 lemon

Preheat oven to 350°; grease and flour ceramic or glass loaf pan. Blend flax seed and water in blender until frothy and set aside. In a large bowl, combine applesauce, tahini, and sweetener; beat in flax seed mixture. Mix in flour, baking powder and salt. Add milk and lemon; mix well. Fold in sunflower seeds and raisins until blended. Pour batter into glass/ceramic loaf pan. Sprinkle sesame seeds evenly on top. Bake approximately 50-60 minutes or until knife inserted in center is clean. Cool in pan 10 minutes; cool completely on rack before slicing. *I pulverize the whole lemon in my blender.

RAW SWEET POTATO PIE

~Filling

3 medium sweet potatoes peeled and cut into chunks

6 pitted dates

⅓ cup raw honey or agave nectar

¼ cup unsweetened shredded coconut

¾ tsp nutmeg

1 tsp fresh lemon juice

1½ tsp cinnamon

3 Tbsp ground walnuts

~Crust

1 cup almonds or walnuts soaked at least 8 hours in pure water/drained

1 cup dates loosely packed

Process dates and almonds in your food processor until a dough forms. Press evenly into pie plate with wet fingers. Run raw sweet potatoes through your masticating* juicer along with 6 dates, using a blank instead of screen. Place in a bowl; mix in remaining ingredients except walnuts. Add filling to crust and cover with ground walnuts. Refrigerate for at least 1 hour. *Masticating vegetable juicers chew or grind veggies; instead of using a spinning basket, it uses gears to grind the produce.

RAW APPLE PIE

~Crust

2 cups walnuts or almonds (or a combination of both) soaked for at least 8 hours in pure water/drained

5 dates

Process nuts and dates in food processor until dough forms; press evenly into pie plate

~Bottom layer

2 sweet apples

Juice from ½ lemon

Process lemon and apples until chunky smooth, spread onto crust

~Top layer

2 sweet apples

1 cup currants or ¾ cup organic raisins

Juice from ½ lemon

1 banana

2 tsp cinnamon

Process all ingredients until applesauce consistency. Spread onto bottom layer, chill and serve. This is a wonderful summer pie, cool, light and delicious.

CAROB CAKE

2 cups whole wheat flour

½ cup white wheat flour

½ cup sorghum flour

½ cup Sucanat (brand name) sugar

½ cup carob powder

2 tsp baking soda

1 tsp pure vanilla extract

$^2/_3$ cup unsweetened apple sauce

2 tsp vinegar

2 cups cold pure water

Preheat oven 350°; oil and flour wide loaf pan or bundt pan. Mix dry ingredients together. Wisk wet ingredients into dry very hard for about 1 minute. Immediately pour batter into prepared pan. Bake 35 minutes or until knife tests clean, cool. Frost with strawberry all natural fruit jam and sprinkle with shredded coconut. Or you might try frosting it with the thick portion of canned all natural coconut milk, mixed with agave nectar to sweeten.

Millet Pudding

Boil 1 cup millet in 2½ cups pure water until softened; cool. In a blender, combine ⅔ cup unsweetened shredded coconut, 1½ cups pure water and 10 pitted dates, blend until creamy. In a large bowl mix together 1 large sweet apple finely chopped, ½ cup chopped walnuts and ½ cup organic raisins. Add blended coconut and millet to bowl; mix well. Chill and enjoy.

Raw Brownies

¼ cup raw flax seed (grind fine in coffee grinder)

¾ cup raw sunflower seeds

1 cup raw almonds

¼ cup raw pumpkin seeds

1 Tbsp raw sesame seeds

15 raw pitted dates

½ cup carob powder

1 tsp blackstrap molasses (unsulphured, optional)

½ cup chopped walnuts (optional)

In a food processor, process almonds and all seeds into a powder. Add dates, carob and molasses, pulse until mixed well. While processor is running, add pure water gradually (approximately ⅓ cup) until a firm dough forms. Place dough in bowl; fold in walnuts. Press into an 8×8″ pan; chill; when firm cut into squares.

~MISCELLANEOUS~

VEGETABLE GRAVY

1 Tbsp extra virgin olive oil

2 large onions chopped

4 celery stalks chopped

4 large cloves garlic quartered

1 large bay leaf

2 tsp powdered thyme

1 tsp powdered sage

1 tsp Italian seasoning

2 tsp natural sea salt (or to taste)

5 cups purified water

Brown onion in oil until caramel colored; add remaining ingredients; cook for approximately 15-20 minutes until the veggies are very soft and the spices have permeated the water. Strain the broth of all solids. Simmer broth on medium heat. In a small bowl add ¼ cup water with 2 rounded Tbsp of white wheat flour. Mix into a paste. Pour paste through a fine strainer while over the broth pot; lower the base of the strainer into the pot while stirring into the strainer. This keeps the lumps at bay. Simmer while stirring until thickened. Add more *paste* depending on desired gravy thickness. Season again if necessary. This goes well with mashed potatoes or my Holiday Stuffing recipe.

GARLIC TOAST OR CROUTONS

Toast until crisp any variety of all natural, whole grain bread. Spread a light layer of organic butter on top. Peel large garlic clove and rub it over the toast. The garlic will whittle down as you rub it over the toast's rough surface. Careful, a little garlic goes a long way. If you toast these well and cut them into cubes, they make great croutons for any salad.

BBQ SAUCE

Mix 2 Tbsp raw unfiltered honey with ½ cup all natural ketchup, 1 tsp natural Worcestershire sauce and ½ tsp garlic powder; mix well. This tastes great with my hot Lentil Loaf, Oven Baked Fries and Gluten *Wheat* Ball recipes.

PRETZELS OR BREAD STICKS

1 pkg dry yeast
1½ cup warm purified water
1 Tbsp honey
1 tsp natural sea salt
2 cups white wheat flour
2 cups whole wheat flour

Toppings–garlic powder, poppy seed, sesame seed, caraway seed, onion flakes, pizza pepper flakes, oregano
Extra virgin olive oil

Mix together all ingredients except oil and toppings. Knead on a floured surface until elastic dough forms. Hand roll into sticks or shape into pretzels. Place on oiled non-aluminum baking sheet. Brush with oil and sprinkle with spices. Bake in a 425° oven for approximately 15 minutes until golden brown. I like to serve these with my Lentil Stew.

Apple Banana Oatmeal

On stove top prepare organic rolled oats to your desired consistency, stir in pure vanilla extract and cinnamon to taste. In a single serve bowl, add ½ sweet apple finely chopped and ½ banana cut into thin rounds. Sprinkle cinnamon on fruit, spoon hot oatmeal on top, and drizzle with raw honey. Serve with almond or rice milk. This makes a great snack too.

Hummus

2 cups cooked garbanzo beans (chick peas)
¼ cup tahini
¼ cup fresh lemon juice
2 large garlic cloves minced
¼ tsp cumin
1 tsp natural sea salt (optional)

Process beans in food processor until thick and creamy; add purified water or cooking liquid from beans to accomplish this. Add the rest of the ingredients and process well. Use as a veggie dip or sandwich spread. I have used 2 cans of great northern beans in place of garbanzo beans with delicious success.

HOLIDAY WASSAIL

1 quart unsweetened all natural apple juice
1 pint unsweetened all natural orange juice
1 pint unsweetened all natural pineapple juice
4 whole cinnamon sticks
1 Tbsp whole cloves

Pour juice and spices into a large crock pot; simmer on high for approximately 2 hours or until the smell of cinnamon and cloves fills your home! This is a Christmas and Thanksgiving tradition in my home. Your guests will enjoy it throughout the holiday season.

FRESH GINGER TEA

Cut and peel a 1" piece of fresh ginger root; steep in a cup of boiling pure water for 5-8 minutes. The longer you steep the ginger the stronger the flavor. Add ½ tsp of raw honey to sweeten if you like. This tea feels lovely on a sore throat. For a longer shelf life, store fresh ginger in the freezer.

Herb Bread (bread machine)

1¼ cup purified water

2 Tbsp extra virgin olive oil

1 tsp natural sea salt

1¾ cup whole wheat flour

1¾ cup white wheat flour

2 tsp raw honey

2 Tbsp dried parsley

1 Tbsp Italian seasoning

1 Tbsp garlic powder

2 tsp onion flakes

2 tsp dry yeast

Place wet or dry ingredients in your machine according to the order your machine requires. Add liquid ingredients to bread pan, and then add dry ingredients excluding the yeast. Make a little well in the flour with your finger and pour the yeast into it. Snap the pan into the machine and close the lid. Bake on *French* setting with a light crust. Any variety of dried herbs you have on hand would work fine in this recipe, the more the better.

Squash Pickles

3 small yellow squash, zucchini or cucumber sliced ⅛" thick

½ cup chopped onion

2 large garlic cloves halved

1 red pepper cut into strips

1½ tsp natural sea salt

¾ cup raw apple cider vinegar

¾ tsp mustard seed

¾ tsp celery seed

¼ tsp dill

¼ tsp dry mustard

Stuff a large glass jar full with the vegetables; add spices and pour vinegar to cover veggies. Seal with a lid and store in refrigerator for 10+ days until desired pickle flavor/texture is achieved.

ALMOND MILK

Soak 1 cup of raw almonds for at least 8 hours or overnight in pure water. In a blender, blend drained almonds, 5 pitted dates and 5 cups purified water. Blend well, until creamy milk is made. Strain in a fine strainer or cheese cloth to remove any small pieces. Store in a glass container in the refrigerator for up to 4 days. Shake well before serving. If you have a small blender, you may need to process this in 2 parts. Add a tsp of real vanilla extract for vanilla milk. If you prefer sweeter milk add more dates. This is surprisingly delicious and oh so nutritious!

ALMOND MILK YOGURT

This recipe takes time . . . mostly waiting.

Dehydrator with temperature control

½ cup starter–100% organic full cream yogurt with *live active* cultures: These friendly bacteria will turn your almond milk into yogurt.

8 cups almond milk (see above)

Candy thermometer

Large glass mason jars

Pour 8 cups almond milk into a large cooking pot. Heat the milk to 185°; use your thermometer to test. Cool milk down to 110°. Cooling can take some time. Speed the process by putting the pot into a sink of cool water. The temperature may drop quickly so have your thermometer ready– 110°! When you've reached 110°, add ½ cup of starter yogurt and stir until dissolved; pour into glass jars and place the lids on. Place them into your dehydrator for 10-12 hours at 100°. Do not disturb the jars. When the yogurt is firm, refrigerate until cold; approximately 12-24 hours. This yogurt will be thinner than traditional yogurt. I enjoy mine with organic raisins, fresh fruit and sunflower seeds. A dollop of natural fruit jam tastes nice too.

Family Fun Recipes

Use bleached, bromated all purpose white flour for these recipes

Homemade Play Dough (for the little ones)

1 cup white flour
½ cup salt (cheap table salt/sodium chloride)
⅓ to ½ cup water (chlorinated tap water)
Food coloring

Add food coloring to water and mix well. In a mixing bowl mix flour and salt together; add water slowly. Mix until dough forms. Add more flour if dough is too sticky. Store in air-tight baggies; will keep approximately 1 month. This can be played with as is or cut into shapes and baked in a 275° oven for approximately 15-20 minutes to harden. Cool and paint or decorate with magic markers. Put a hole in the top before baking to make ornaments, beads and jewelry.

PAPER MACHE' (FOR OLDER CHILDREN)

Make a thin paste (like applesauce) by mixing white flour and water together. Dip strips of newspaper into the paste and drape over an inflated balloon or cardboard/wire structure, cover completely. Allow to dry thoroughly; paint. Use colorful wrapping paper in place of newspaper for a different effect. I used to love to do this as a kid. It's super fun, but messy!

So then, whether you eat or drink,
or whatever you may do, do all for
the honor and glory of God.

1 Corinthians 10:31

SHOPPING GUIDE

Vegetables *artichoke *asparagus *avocado *brussels sprout *broccoli *cabbage *carrots *cauliflower *celery *organic corn *cucumber *dark green lettuce *eggplant *garlic *ginger root *green beans *green onion *green pepper *hot peppers *kale *mushroom *olives *onion *orange peppers *mustard greens *parsley *parsnips *potatoes *sweet potato *radishes *red pepper *romaine lettuce *rutabagas *spaghetti squash *spinach *spring mix *acorn squash *swiss chard *tomato *turnips & greens *cherry tomato *yellow pepper *zucchini squash

Fruit *apple *apricot *banana *blackberries *blueberries *cantaloupe *casaba melon *cherries *coconut *cranberries *grapes *grapefruit *figs * kiwi *honeydew melon *kumquat *lemon *lime *mango *nectarine *dates *dried fruit (no sulphur dioxide) *watermelon *tangelos *oranges *papaya *peaches *pear *persimmon *pineapple *plumb *pomegranate *raspberries *strawberries

Whole Grains *whole grain pasta and noodles *brown rice *bulgur wheat *barley *millet *oat bran *steel cut oats *quinoa *organic rolled oats *wild rice *all natural rice and grain mixes *wheat gluten *whole wheat flour *sorghum flour *whole wheat pastry flour *white wheat flour (unbleached-unbromated) *whole grain corn meal (non GMO) *whole grain all natural pancake and waffle mix *whole grain all natural boxed cereal (no BHT) *whole grain all natural tortilla wraps *all natural 100% whole grain bread

Miscellaneous *dried beans *all natural canned beans (no sodium) *dried lentils *raw nuts and seeds *flax seed *unsweetened coconut shreds or flakes *organic raisins *first cold pressed extra virgin olive oil *raw vinegar *fresh and dried herbs *nutritional yeast flakes *low sodium tamari *sesame tahini *almond butter *all natural sea salt *dry yeast *all natural vegetable broth (low sodium) *organic popcorn *agave nectar *Sucanat (brand name) sugar *carob powder *all natural hot pepper sauce *all natural unsweetened applesauce *baking powder (non-aluminum) *all natural mayonnaise, ketchup, Dijon and yellow mustard *all natural salsa *canned all natural crushed tomato (low sodium) *blackstrap molasses (unsulphured) *raw unfiltered honey *natural fruit jam/jelly *herbal tea (no caffeine)

~ Make a copy of this guide and keep it with you for easy shopping!

A RELATIONSHIP
WITH YOUR CREATOR

Earlier I mentioned that there is only one race, the human race and we are all descendants of Adam and Eve (Acts 17:26). God shows no partiality (favoritism) and we are all equal in His eyes; man, woman, young, old, black and white (Acts 10:34). There are, however, only two kinds of people in this sense – those who have received Jesus as their Lord and Savior and those who have rejected Him (Matthew 12:30). Our mighty Creator has breathed the breath of life into each of us, this is the *real* us, our spirit man (Genesis 2:7; 1 Corinthians 15:44; 45). We were supposed to live forever with Him and enjoy the God (Creator) and human (created) relationship. Unfortunately, our original parents–created with free will–chose to disobey God by sinning (Genesis 3:11). Sin has led us to an eternity without God and sin is the reason for death and suffering in the world. You see, our awesome Creator is so Holy that our sin separates us from Him (Isaiah 59:2; Romans 3:23). Genesis describes how hurt God was over man's choice to disobey. God is not mocked. They reaped what they sowed then, and we reap what we sow today (Galatians 6:7).

But God missed His intimate relationship with man and the original way He intended it. He loved us too much to leave it that way. So, He sent His one and only Son–Emmanuel "God with us" (Matthew 1:23; Isaiah 7:14). That's why we celebrate Christmas. On the cross, Jesus suffered the punishment for our sin and bought our spirits back from an eternity in hell (John 3:16). His blood was shed to cover and cleanse us from *all* sin (Romans 6:23; Hebrews 9:22, 26, 28). Graciously, our risen Lord's gift of salvation (Easter) has bridged the gap between Holy God and sinful man.

Jesus Christ is the only way to restore our relationship with our Creator (1 Timothy 2:5; 1 Peter 3:18; Romans 5:8-11; John 14:6). We simply need to receive this free gift of salvation (John 1:12; Romans 10:9-10). This is the most important relationship of all and is the key toward our healing and the restoration of our relationships. It is the answer to wholeness, balance and peace of mind, body and spirit. If you *choose* to receive Him right now, please pray this prayer . . .

Dear Lord Jesus, I know that I am a sinner and I ask for your forgiveness. I believe that You died for my sins and rose from the dead. I turn away from my sins and invite you to come into my heart and life. I want to serve and trust you as my Lord and Savior. I want to be led by your Holy Spirit in all things. In your precious Name I pray. Amen.

You sincerely prayed the prayer – Now what? Rejoice! Your name is written in the Lamb's book of life! (Revelation 3:5-6; 20:15). When your breath (your spirit, the real you) leaves your body, you will be present with your Savior Jesus Christ in Heaven (2 Corinthians 5:8; John 14:1-3).

The next thing you'll need to do is purchase a Bible (God's Holy Word). The New International Version (NIV) is a good one to begin with. I prefer a parallel Bible of the King James Version and the Amplified Version. Try to read the Bible every day; this is your spiritual food. The book of John in the New Testament is a good place to start.

Find a church home. This may take some time as you pray and decide where you will be fed spiritually. Look for a church that teaches the full Gospel and for a minister who uses the Bible, so that you can follow along in your own. If a church you visit says–or does–anything contrary to the Word of God, move on. The Holy Spirit, Who now indwells you, will lead you to the right church by an *inner knowing* and peace (1 Corinthians 2:12-13; 3:16).

~ Join your church home and get involved in your area of giftedness (your God-given abilities).

~ Pray (This is how you talk to Jesus.)

~ Read the Word of God (This is how He will speak to you.)

~ Listen to scripturally inspired music

~ Fellowship with other believers in and outside of church

~ Represent Jesus here on earth with love, balance and good health in mind, body and spirit

~ Share with others the good news of Jesus Christ and what He has done for you (your testimony)

"Who shall ever separate us from Christ's love? Shall suffering and affliction and tribulation? Or calamity and distress? Or persecution or hunger or destitution or peril or sword? Yet amid all these things we are more than conquerors and gain a surpassing victory through Him Who loved us. For I am persuaded beyond doubt (am sure) that neither death nor life, nor angels nor principalities, nor things impending and threatening nor things to come, nor powers, nor height nor depth, nor anything else in all creation will be able to separate us from the love of God which is in Christ Jesus our Lord."

Romans 8:35, 37-39

CONCLUSION

The Lord has taken me through this twenty year journey to teach me many things. I am certain you have seen yourself or even someone you may know on these pages. Scripture tells us that *they overcame* the enemy by the blood of the Lamb (Jesus' sacrifice on the cross) and by the word of their testimony (Revelation 12:11). It is my sincere hope that my testimony will guide you to a healthy lifestyle, healthy mindset and an eternity with your Creator. The very next moment is new to you. What will you choose? Choose life!

"Beloved, I pray above all things that you may prosper and be in health, even as your soul prospers."

3 John 2

If anything in this book has had a positive impact on your life, I would love to hear from you. Please email me at tendingthetemple.trish@gmail.com

To order www.createspace.com/3494411

Made in the USA
Middletown, DE
24 January 2015